To

Debora

from

Florence and Vida

October 1974

The Getting Game

The
Getting
Game

George Daniels

Illustrations by the author

HARPER & ROW, PUBLISHERS

New York, Evanston, San Francisco, London

FIRST EDITION

Designed by Janice Stern

Library of Congress Cataloging in Publication Data

Daniels, George Emery, 1914-
    The getting game.
     1. Secondhand trade.   2. Junk trade.   I. Title.
HF5482.D35   381   73-14251
ISBN 0-06-010939-4

To Gooni, who helped all the way

Contents

The Getting Game

You'd Better Believe It

Maybe you'd like to live in the grand manner. You dream about a palatial country estate with rolling lawns, marble halls, and crystal chandeliers. On a sparkling summer morning you stroll across the tree-shaded courtyard to the big, rambling garage to select a car, perhaps a Rolls, for a spin to the shore and a day on your yacht. And on those frosty winter weekends you skate for a while on one of your frozen gazing pools. Then you loll by the big log fire in your rosewood-paneled drawing room, highball in hand, while your mate serenades you from one of the grand pianos in the music room. It's all yours, free and clear. No payments to make, no mortgages to meet. Just yours, lock, stock, and barrel.

If this sort of life appeals to you, the chances are you can have it on your present income, whatever it is. (That's where this book comes in.) But you can't be a conformist.

Unless you are wildly wealthy you simply do not acquire such lavish possessions in the conventional fashion. But you do not steal them. It is neither proper nor practical to steal things like country mansions and grand pianos. There are better ways of getting them for little or nothing, each an adventure in itself. You may not believe this, of course. Most people don't. We didn't either, until we took title to our first Rolls-Royce, a beautiful, glistening, perfect thing, without spending a cent. (The chapter titled "A Choice of Rolls-Royce" tells the story.) Since then people have often implored us to accept houses and yachts and all kinds of things, either for nothing or for a very few dollars.

Summer before last, a perfect stranger drove up to the house and gave us a trailer simply because he had heard we wanted one and didn't feel like buying it. He wouldn't take a penny for it. He wouldn't even take a drink. He just signed the thing over to us, parked it at the end of the driveway, and drove away happy as a lark. Last summer we gave a Buick to a young man who had mentioned several times that he liked Buicks when he could get them free or nearly free. It was quite a nice one, with all the fancy extras including automatic transmission, and it ran like a top.

The only thing incredible about these giveaways is the fact that they're not incredible at all. They make perfect sense to all concerned when they occur. (More about this later in the book.) The important point to note is that in both cases mentioned, the recipient had spread the

word that he wanted the thing involved and wanted it cheap or gratis. If you want something and can't afford it, or you simply don't feel like paying for it, tell everybody that. Then find out as much as you can about the thing you want. Those are two primary rules of the Getting Game. The results can be amazing.

Some years ago, for example, we wanted a grand

3

piano, and our budget couldn't even stand a ukulele. So we told everybody that if we ever found a grand piano for the price of a pair of shoes, we'd snap it up. We told our friends, our neighbors, our favorite bartenders, and the cop on the beat, a fine fellow who drove a radio patrol car. Then we wangled a tour through a piano factory. (This was easy, as many manufacturers like to take people on tours of their factories to show them how nicely they put things together.)

We needed the grand piano more or less because of the house we had at the time. It was a lovely ten-room Dutch colonial with 150 acres, a private bridge over a river, an outdoor dance floor, a beautiful carriage shed, a private lake, and a living room that was forty feet long and twenty feet wide, with two fireplaces. The place was, of course, much too big for the handful of furniture we owned, but it was the only thing we could rent for less than a one-room apartment. (How this came about is explained in the chapter titled "If You Can't Join It, Rent It.") As the living room didn't have much in it aside from a couple of rolling bars and a sofa, we figured a grand piano would go a long way toward giving it a lived-in look.

Not long after the piano-factory tour, our police friend called to us one morning from his patrol car to say he had run across a grand piano that seemed interesting. Its owner, a millionaire, was afraid to go near it, as were a lot of other people. But it might be just right for us.

From what he said, and from other things we had heard at the piano factory, we felt we should carry an ax with us when we went to see the piano, and it's a good thing we did. Without it we might never have gotten a $4,000 concert grand for $20. But we got it and everybody was delighted, including the millionaire and a number of his friends. There were a few tense moments at the outset, though, like the night when the living room was filled with hundreds of piano keys and whiskey glasses and people singing. We still have the piano despite the fact that musically inclined folk, including the piano tuner, have offered us all kinds of money for it. The important thing to remember if you want a grand piano is that you can probably get one the same way, maybe for nothing. We know other people who have done it, and a few who shudder at the thought of it. You'll find the details in the chapter titled "Steinway in the Snow."

One of the other major factors in playing the Getting Game successfully lies in learning strange sources for things and never turning your nose up at any of them. Right now, for instance, you are very likely within easy driving distance of at least one of the greatest bargain centers on the face of the earth, a building wrecker's headquarters. This is a strange realm where men have made millions by working for nothing and lost millions by bad-guessing the weather, and where you can often buy a house for the price of a color TV. Some people go into ecstasy when they see one of these places. Others actually go into shock. We introduced a young bride to one a couple of years ago, and in less than two minutes she was flailing her arms around like a maniac and screaming and yelling with tears running down her face. And she had a good reason. All the way home in the car she kept muttering that people shouldn't do such horrible things. Then she'd look back at the enormous truck behind us and laugh in a hollow, mindless way. "Just wait till Harry finds out!" she kept saying. "Just you wait!"

All this resulted from her learning that house wreckers destroy salvaged items that they can't sell. On that particular occasion, a bulldozer was squashing things like furniture and pianos, and was about to squash the one musical instrument in the place that our bride friend regarded as an absolute treasure, and, of course, she considered this a horrible thing to do. Business reasons notwithstanding. So she stopped the procedure with such depth of feeling as to disrupt the entire management. Then, when she discovered that the treasure she had rescued was priced at only $20 instead of the hundreds she had expected, she spent a minute recovering from the shock, and then bought the thing. In fact it was being delivered to her house in the enormous truck that she kept looking at behind us.

Harry was her husband, and on that same Saturday afternoon he found out what his bride had done when he walked into their house and discovered that her new acquisition was the biggest thing in the living room. But she had not forgotten Harry, either. During her ordeal of the afternoon she had spotted a treasure for him too. And when he heard about it, he did something that few people in the world have ever done or even thought of doing. He took his bride back to the same wrecking yard, followed her into an isolated shed, and bought a hurdy-gurdy. All of which is detailed in Chapter 3.

Neither of them will ever be the same again. But they're happy. Happier than they ever dreamed of being before. We have encountered them many times since then, always in that mad bargain center, wandering around grinning, with a glazed look in their eyes.

Lots of strange things happen in those places. Once, when we took a very earnest geologist and his wife to one of them to get some granite gargoyles, a live mule came out of the wall and stood staring at us, beside a marble statue of Julius Caesar. We learned later that the mule was indeed famous, and had spent the night in jail in Tarrytown, New York. But the geologist and his wife got their gargoyles at a price so fantastically low they're still talking about it twenty-five years later. The fact that the whole thing took place in the ballroom under a former Yonkers speakeasy amazes them even now.

Most of these places have at least a million or more individual items for sale. We bought a two-headed stuffed calf and an outboard motor in one and still got change from a twenty-dollar bill. A friend of ours bought an elevator and a bathroom in another one for about the price of a new suit, and was puzzled to find that in the same place three doorknobs from New York's old Ritz Carlton cost just as much as the elevator. All of which makes the shopping fascinating. If you'd like this kind of thing, and you should because it pays, you'll find out all about it in the chapter titled "Damn the Pipe Organs—the Kitchens Are Coming!"

Sometimes it's not the bargain price that's so startling, but the thing itself, and it may not come from a bargain counter. It was that way with one of our favorite cars, a three-ton canary-yellow convertible twenty-three feet long, with mahogany trim. You could cruise all day in it at 120 miles an hour if you owned a racetrack. But we were much more interested in its luxury than its speed.

The first time we drove it was one of those occasions you never forget. It was a blistering hot August day, so hot that the asphalt on the roadway was actually getting sticky in spots, when we started down Main Street in Greenwich. The traffic was crawling around a big truck that had boiled over, and finally everything stopped altogether for a brief period. This gave me and my wife a chance to scrape some of the ice from our windshield before things got rolling again. As we scraped we noticed that the man in the car beside us was staring as if he had never seen an automobile before. He stayed as close to us as possible as we moved on, and when we nosed into a parking space in front of our pet liquor store he parked right next to us. He could not figure out, he said, how come we were scraping ice off the windshield on such a helluva hot day. I explained that we had to scrape it off or we couldn't see where we were going. As soon as I said it I realized it wasn't a very complete answer, but between the water squirting out of the side of the car and the smoke pouring out of the trunk, his attention was distracted anyway. There was really nothing at all wrong, but the car was a bit odd—odd enough to find its way into TV and the newsreels. We didn't get this one free, however. It cost almost as much as a new refrigerator. If you'd like one similar to it (we drove it a delightful 90,000 miles), you'll find all the details in the chapter titled "The Car on the Barroom Floor."

When you become really proficient at the Getting Game you'll find yourself doing things that seem perfectly normal to you but not to anybody else. For instance, you might be driving very slowly along a lovely country road and gazing up at the utility wires. Somebody might ask you why you're doing it, and you might answer that it's the only way you can decide whether or not to buy a roomy old farmhouse for $50. This might be a perfectly sensible answer. (We know because we took a ride like that and didn't buy the house.) But it sounds pretty crazy to most people. When it all works out right, however, you can end up with an unbelievable bargain. A fisherman we used to know bought a restaurant that way for a couple of hundred dollars one afternoon, and had it going great guns the next day. In fact, it was the only place in the area that served whale meat. If you like prices like this, you'll be very interested in the chapter titled "The House That Came to Dinner."

You finally reach a stage where nobody believes anything you say about how you get things. Then you lie about it all. (This is covered in the chapter titled "How to Lie About a Buy.") We have to lie aplenty, even when people drop in at the house. The house is roughly eighty feet long, with seven rooms, two baths, kitchen, laundry, and assorted patios and terraces, along with a waterfall and a garage full of boats. Altogether it would have cost about the same as our station wagon if we hadn't gotten the station wagon so cheap.

What confuses things somewhat is the fact that the house, though only about twenty years old, is a hundred years older at one end than the other. And the old end is the new end—which contains an air-conditioned dining room. Against the east wall of the dining room stands a handsome olivewood sideboard with an Italian marble top and an antique lock that can be opened only with a broken key. Naturally, this is a conversation piece and people ask where we got it. We used to say we found it in an antique shop for $25, but nobody believed it. One of them went so far as to bring us a furniture catalog to prove that even ordinary factory-made sideboards of comparable size cost six times as much. So now we say it cost $100, and, of course, that isn't true either. The plain fact is that it cost 80 cents and it came from a superhighway,

We bought the lumber for the century-old end of our
house here for $46. It had been a blacksmith shop.

a cheese factory, and a swamp. But you can't tell people
things like that. You'll find out about it in the "Damn the
Pipe Organs" chapter.

At the north end of the same room there's a delicately
ornate wood stove more than a century old, and it fasci-
nates antique fanciers. We didn't buy this one at all. It
was given to us, and for a while we told the truth about
that. Just for a while. We explained honestly that it was

a gift from an old friend and sword collector who had a horse-drawn hearse on his roof, but no horse to go with it. He often told us that this situation irked him, so eventually we presented him with a big, colorful, red-eyed horse that had feathers on its head. When he put it on the roof it kicked like mad and did other things that caused a tempest in the neighborhood. But this part of the affair is not involved with our dining room. As you will read elsewhere in this book, our friend eventually triumphed. But even before that, he presented us with our beautiful wood stove because we admired it among his wood stove collection long before the colorful horse with the feathered head ever flashed its big red eyes. There is a nuance in all of this that should not be overlooked: you get to know unusual and wonderful people when you play the Getting Game. This is often as much fun as the Getting part of the game—in the long run, more fun. All in all, it's a topnotch sport that comes naturally, and everybody wins.

A Choice of Rolls-Royce

Our free Rolls-Royce Affair began when a friend of ours stopped by to show us the big elaborate hearse he had just bought for $75 to use at his country place. He said he felt like a kid with a new toy, because he had been hankering for a hearse ever since his younger days during Prohibition, when the family bootlegger used to deliver liquor in one. But, of course, that was long ago, and this hearse was for an entirely different purpose. It was just what he needed for hauling power mowers to the repair shop, and picking up shrubs from the nursery, and even grocery shopping. Also, he planned to remodel the inside of the thing so he could use it as a station wagon to pick up guests from the train when he threw a big party. In fact, it was the driver of one of the private cabs down at the railroad station who had told him about the used-car dealer with the hearses.

The way our friend explained it all, if you're going to buy a car new it should be something racy that you can have fun with, not something humdrum like a pickup truck. And if you buy a pickup truck secondhand, it's likely to be in worse shape than a secondhand hearse, because funerals just don't bang around at sixty miles an hour. Which seemed to make a certain amount of sense. And, since he knew we were thinking about building a house, he thought maybe we ought to get down to this special used-car dealer and grab a hearse before they were all gone. Of course, the dealer also had regular cars too. Things like our convertible. In fact, our friend's wife had also bought a car there, which she was at that moment driving up to the country place. So maybe if we mentioned all this, the dealer would give us a little extra break.

It may have been this possibility that prompted us to go there, since our convertible had a peculiar top which was likely to become more peculiar at any time. The trouble was that it sagged, and whenever we were caught in heavy rain and heavy traffic at the same time, it filled up with water like an overhead reservoir, which made it bulge down and tap people on the head. There was also an element of suspense in the mildewed area just behind the windshield, which dripped when the top was full of water, and gave the impression that the whole thing might let go.

To overcome this problem, we had developed certain maneuvers for emptying the top, the simplest of which was merely zigzagging gently as we drove along. This created a sort of tidal action in the reservoir and sloshed out most of the water, first from one side, then from the other. It called for a certain sense of rhythm, however, and naturally could not be carried out under the eyes of the constabulary. So we had come to the conclusion that what we really needed was another top or another car. And maybe our hearse-buying friend's dealer would be a good place to start looking.

As things turned out, it started to rain while we were on our way to the place the next day, and since the traffic was heavy and we had a patrol car right behind us, we couldn't use our tidal maneuver. So the top was full and dripping when we pulled into the parking space at the used-car lot. And it let go altogether just as a salesman in a raincoat started walking toward us.

This, in case you have never seen it happen, is something of a spectacle. As the top rips loose from the windshield, it flaps down over your face and chutes a deluge of water into your lap, after which it drains in little streams under the doors. And, instinctively, you open the doors and step out into the rain, which, at that point, is more comfortable than the car.

As we did that, the salesman, who was headed toward us anyway, smiled sympathetically and said maybe we would like to sell the car, which somehow struck me funny. I said, "Sure, just give me a Rolls-Royce and a hundred bucks, and you can take it away," which I thought was a funny answer, although it didn't get a laugh out of the salesman. He just said he'd be right back, and went into the little plywood office with the USED CARS sign on top. And although we were still a little jangled by our unexpected bath, we recovered our senses enough to follow him toward the office instead of simply standing there in the rain. But before we got there, he was on his way back, smiling genially. He walked around our drenched convertible, climbed into the wet seat, flipped the top behind his head, and started the motor. "It's a deal," he said. "Bertie can help you pick out a Rolls."

It was probably because we looked confused that the salesman asked, "A Rolls-Royce and a hundred bucks— that's what you said, wasn't it?" (This was our first experience with a basic rule of the Getting Game: if you want something and don't feel like paying for it, tell people.)

I remember that things seemed a little unreal at that moment and got even more unreal when a tall thin man turned up from somewhere holding an umbrella over my wife's head and said, with a British accent, that he hoped her legs weren't too long or too short. Then he turned to me and said he could see that my legs were just about right. "You can't adjust the front seat in the limousines," he added.

This, we learned, was Bertie, who handled the funeral cars, in this case big black Rolls-Royce limousines. "I never saw so many Rolls-Royces at one time," I told him, as I looked at the row of them lined up at the rear of the lot.

"Rolls-Royce," was Bertie's only reply.

So I told him that was what I had said. Rolls-Royces. And he explained gently, "One may refer to several Cadillacs, or several dump trucks, but one does not refer to several Rolls-Royces. One refers to several Rolls-Royce." As they were all alike, we simply selected the one that happened to be fifth from the end because we happened to like the number. And, of course, we were given a demonstration, by a man in white overalls named something that sounded like Zunk, who showed us how everything worked, and other unrelated but interesting things.

"These things ain't just for stuffed shirts," he said. "They can really roll, and they don't make no noise."

He was particularly insistent that we see the gleaming, polished engine, which he told us was called a Silver Ghost. "Looks like one of them things in Tiffany's window," he said.

But just as important as the mechanical fine points, in Zunk's estimation, were the psychological effects. "With one of these things all you gotta do is wave at the guy at the gate and you can drive into all them fancy clubs," he said. "But you gotta play it right."

As Zunk explained it, if you happen to dent a fender and you want to get it smoothed out cheap, you wear a chauffeur's cap when you take it to a body shop. And you say you have to pay for the damage out of your own pocket because the boss would fire you if he knew you

17

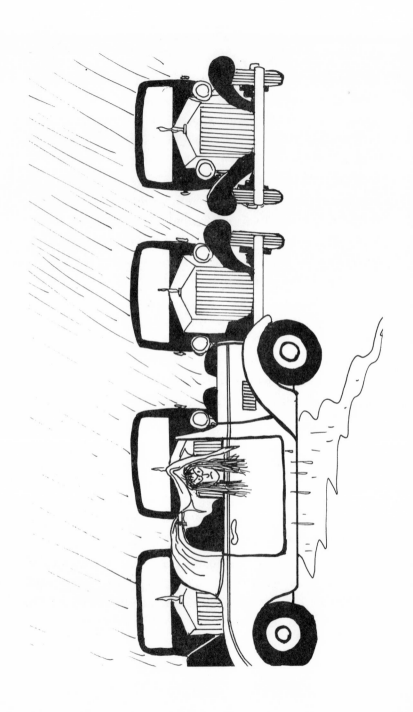

had creased his Rolls. But when you want attention like having your tires checked or your windshield cleaned, you should become the boss and smoke a big cigar if you like cigars, because chauffeurs just ain't allowed to smoke cigars.

When we bade farewell to Zunk and started home with our limousine and hundred-dollar profit, my wife took a turn at the wheel so I could sample the comfort of riding in back. After we changed places I stopped for gas to make sure the gauge worked, and as the rain had stopped, I got out for another look at the Rolls. The station attendant asked the usual "Fill 'er up?" and I said a couple bucks' worth would be enough. Which prompted him to ask how come a babe like the one I was driving for, who could ride around in a rig like that, would get a couple of bucks' worth of gas. So I tried Zunk's technique, and said her husband owned one of the biggest oil companies in the country and got sore as hell if I filled the tank anyplace but in one of his own stations.

Then my wife came into the front seat beside me, gave me a kiss, and said, "Home, James." And the attendant gave me change for a five, winked, and walked away.

When we showed our Rolls to our friend with the hearse, he told us we were lucky. His wife had one, and the cab driver at the railroad station up in the country had one. And, since they were selling for $150 apiece, they'd probably all be gone in a few days. To his way of

If you can't find a real Rolls at a price you like, maybe an imitation like this on your Volkswagen will do.

thinking it was a lot better than paying seven or eight hundred dollars for a new convertible, which was the going price for one in our size range at the time. And he was sure we'd never see a Rolls for less.

And we didn't. In fact, when we finally parted with ours, it brought $500. And we often wish we had it back.

It's one of the models wealthy collectors value as a classic. And the last one we came across was priced at $125,000. But you can still often swap something newer and more rakish for an older but handsome limousine. Possibly a Cadillac, and with luck, maybe a Rolls, even today. And if you can't find what you want at the usual sources and all you want is a bargain, you can always call the undertaker.

If You Want to Try It

A used Rolls-Royce costs more now than when we managed to get ours for nothing. But then, everything costs more now. Like those martinis that used to be 35 cents in a really posh nightclub and now cost about five times as much almost anywhere.

Today, if you find an oldish Rolls that needs some work done on it, you might be able to make a deal for as little as the price of a new Ford. (So, if you have something expensive to trade, you could still get your car free.) Otherwise your used Rolls might now cost as much as a small house, which is easier on the budget than a new Rolls, which costs as much as a fairly large house. Depending on where the house might be. The confusing part of it is that a really old

Rolls frequently costs more than a brand-new one, if it happens to be one of the prized types. In a way, they're like real estate. The longer you keep them, the more they're worth, if you wait long enough.

People who deal in new and used foreign cars are a good bet as a starting point, as are Rolls dealers, of course. But you have to do some scouting. Not all dealers have used ones on hand. After all, it isn't a car that was built by the millions, like most of the ones we go shopping to find. Only about sixty thousand have been built since 1904, and more than half of them are still on the road. So not many Rolls owners are likely to feel like selling. And if you manage to locate one that's for sale, and you can afford to buy, you'd better grab it. It shouldn't cost much to run. Our limousine averaged around fourteen miles on a gallon of regular on the open road, back when gas sold for about 15 cents a gallon. And it's probably still on the road somewhere, getting the same mileage.

Damn the Pipe Organs—
the Kitchens Are Coming!

If you'd like to buy an elevator cheap, or a washtub full of bifocals, or a smashed airplane, or maybe a couple thousand dollars' worth of lumber for a few hundred dollars, there are places where you can do it. Probably within the next half hour. But for some of the things, you have to be there at the right time.

We first learned about all this some years back, just after we started building our house. We were driving along the Post Road in Greenwich when we happened to notice that a mansion was missing and several men were walking out of the driveway that had led to the mansion, carrying a beautiful stairway, which they loaded carefully into the last in a line of parked trucks.

We decided to pull up behind the truck, which was a big ten-wheeler that already contained a pile of timbers and stained-glass windows, and other things like a huge credenza, a harpsichord, and several bathtubs, one of which was occupied by a man eating his lunch. (If you try it, you will find that a big empty bathtub is a very comfortable place for lunch.)

We asked what had happened to the mansion and where the truck was going with the stairway and everything. One of the men answered that they had just finished tearing the place down, and the stuff in the truck was going back to what he called the yard. "If you want to buy anything," he said, nodding toward the biggest bulldozer we had ever seen, "talk to the boss."

We watched the boss, a big distinguished-looking man in an expensively tailored business suit, as he climbed down from the bulldozer, straightened his tie, and eased into a waiting Cadillac with all the trimmings.

We were in the process of building a house, we told him, and we wondered if we could buy any of the things in the truck—things like the stairway and maybe some windows. "Buy anything you want," he said. "I've got millions of 'em."

How did he happen to be running the bulldozer?

"It cost me three times as much as the Cadillac," he told us. "So I might as well enjoy it."

That was our first contact with the realm of the building wrecker, probably the greatest bargain source on the face of the earth—if you know your way, and aren't the hesitant type. If you visit a wrecking yard and see hundreds of beautiful ladderback chairs in a pile twenty feet high, don't stop to figure out why they're priced at 50 cents apiece. Just grab while the grabbing's good. (We bought six. Thirty minutes later there were none. Which indicates why you must sometimes be in these places at the right time.) At some wreckers' you can leave word with the office manager to call you when a particular item turns up. This might be something like rosewood paneling at 10 cents a foot, or a balalaika or an automatic oil burner. This was the way, for $35, we bought the $300 air conditioner that cools the century-old end of our house.

When you merely browse, of course, you often find nonstandard things for which you may not have any immediate need. But it may be wise to buy anyway in case you are ever shopping for the man who has everything. A few years ago, for example, we bought an old fortune-telling machine with a life-sized wax fortune teller in it for $15 and later found it was an ideal birthday present for an old friend who didn't happen to have one. (The wrecker acquired it during the demolition of a carnival warehouse.)

The explanation for the wrecker's strange wares and prices often lies partly in the way wrecking contracts are written, and partly in the nature of the business itself. A typical wrecking contract gives the wrecker title to everything on the premises when the wrecking job begins, even including the shrubbery. So wreckers suddenly find themselves in possession of such things as live pigs,

laboratory skeletons, old cannons, geese, and goldfish.

One major East Coast wrecker, arriving with his crew at seven in the morning to start razing a palatial home, found a shapely blonde still asleep on one of the divans, after the preceding night's farewell party. "Maybe under the contract I had title to her," he told us, "but I have no place to store things like that."

And storage is a problem. So prices are low to keep things moving, and you can save 50 percent on used lumber, maybe a lot more, especially if you buy a load directly at the wrecking site. That's how we built our studio for $46 and our garage for $27. But, of course, wreckers' prices change with the times like grocery prices and everything else. The last time we checked, our garage would have cost almost as much as a week's groceries. More about this in Chapter 8.

When something just doesn't sell, wreckers have to haul it off to the dump or get rid of it some other way to make room for incoming things. Before air pollution became a problem, they simply burned it up, and often used the heat from blazing furniture to melt the lead out of cast-iron drain pipes.

It was this procedure that got us involved in a sort of nightmare when we took that young bride of two weeks (Chapter 1) to a wrecker's yard for the first time. She was a real music lover who had played the church organ on Sundays since she was a kid, somewhere out West. And she had told my wife how she'd love to keep on play-

Where the gargoyles came from. Once a famous inn,
this is now the headquarters of a major building
wrecker. Building is topped by golden horse weathervane in memory of the company mascot.

ing now that she was married if she could only afford an
organ, which she couldn't.

So we took her to a wrecker's warehouse where we remembered seeing a pretty little pipe organ from some
demolished theater. But it had been moved out to the
storage yard to make room for a dozen kitchens from

some apartment building that was being leveled. And, just as we got there, a bulldozer was grinding toward it for the final shove into a roaring inferno that already was consuming a piano and a pile of furniture, along with the usual array of drainpipe.

The little bride cut loose with such wild waving and screeching and howling that the bulldozer driver stopped short and jumped down to see if he had run over something, like possibly her entire family. The overall result was that the office manager ran out of the warehouse and paled at the sight of our shocked and weeping companion, and we explained that she was interested in the organ. So he had some of the yard workers carry the thing inside and plug it in so she could try it out, which she did by sitting on a nail barrel and running through a full-blast rendition of the "Marseillaise." This bolstered her spirits to the point where she asked the manager, who was already visibly shaken, what the price of the organ was, and he told her $20. Then, as she seemed about to faint, he looked at us in desperation and told her he would give her a piano bench with it and deliver it all free if she lived within ten miles.

We finally got her out of the place, along with the organ, which was loaded onto a big flatbed truck. On the way out we passed the rows of beautiful automatic electric ranges that were arriving from the apartment job, and bought one (which we still have) for $12. And the bride spotted a colorful flower-decorated hurdy-gurdy that she said was just what her husband, Harry, had been looking for ever since she first met him, and he should have it even though it was tagged at twice as much as her pipe organ. Everything worked out fine in the end. Harry found out about the hurdy-gurdy and bought it, which is an experience few people ever have.

Needless to say, it does not pay to be too shaken about what you may see in one of these places. Our nextdoor neighbor, for example, bought a batch of lavish kitchen equipment from one such emporium because he refused to be distracted by the presence of a squirming boa constrictor in a big glass case and a couple of caged lion cubs. Another of our neighbors was more squeamish, however. She missed a chance to buy a beautiful automatic electric range just like ours for the same price because she was unnerved by the sight of a barrel of false teeth and a couple of human skulls on a table under which a man was crawling and rolling a cannonball. People vary. When an artist friend of ours heard about it, he bought the skulls. And there was a logical explanation for it all, anyway. The man who wanted the cannonballs had to crawl under the table to get them from behind a foot locker of lead pipe. And he rolled them out because they were too heavy to lift unless he could stand up, which he couldn't do under the table. It was as simple as that.

It's also important to select your wrecker according to the kind of thing you want to buy. Pick a city wrecker

Berkshire Building Wreckers, bordering on open country, is a good source of wagons and country home furnishings, including antique wood stoves, like the century-old one in our dining room. (Owner of this wrecking company gave it to us in return for the red-eyed mechanical horse we built for his roof.)

for city things like elevators or big steel girders. If you are building a house, you might want a big steel girder so your basement won't have to have a row of posts down the middle. For suburban things like roll-up garage doors and everyday house parts, go to a suburban wrecker. At one of these, for example, we bought seven beautiful old casement windows for $3.50 and two bathrooms for less than the price of a new bathtub. If you want something farmish like wagon wheels, you need a wrecker who reaches into that kind of country. We bought a pair of big beautiful slim-spoked steel wheels and an axle from some kind of an old farm machine for $5, and built a garden cart with that colorful Sicilian look you just don't find in garden carts.

If you're an antique fancier, a wrecker in any area may be a gold mine where you're likely to meet your favorite antique dealer rummaging around. We have an ornate century-old wood stove in our dining room, for example, that would have cost us $12.50 if we had bought it. But we received it as a gift several years ago from the wrecker mentioned in Chapter 1, who had the horse-drawn hearse displayed on his roof, and for whom, as old friends, we provided a suitable horse to go with the hearse. Now antique wood stoves like ours are selling for more than $100.

If you should ever want to make a horse like the one that got us the wood stove, you need an old taffy-pulling machine and an electric motor, both of which, in our case, were provided by the wrecker. The cranks on the taffy machine pushed and pulled wooden rods that moved the legs and the flowing Dynel tail of the plywood horse we put together on the terrace behind our house. And, as the taffy machine ran very fast with no taffy to pull, the horse kicked its legs and flapped its tail at a rate that drew considerable attention from passersby. This, coupled with the fact that it had electrically flashing red eyes and a rotating crown of orange feathers on its head from an old liquor-store display, proved very disturbing to local residents.

The entire matter was eventually resolved when the horse fell off the roof as the result of a severe windstorm and our friend sold the hearse at a tidy profit. Of course, you need not become involved in horsebuilding to acquire an antique wood stove from a wrecker, as you can simply buy one if you are willing to pay the price.

Live horses, too, have been acquired by wreckers in their everyday activities. But it was a mule that became a legend in the business. A New York wrecker who thought it would make a good company mascot bought it sight unseen for $50 from a man who described the mule as young, but neglected to mention that it was dying of a wide variety of mule afflictions.

Delivered by pickup truck to the wrecker's Yonkers headquarters, the mule was too weak to stand up, and had to be carried by the wrecking crew to a big four-poster bed in one of the warehouse furniture storerooms, where it remained for many weeks while its new owner spent several thousand dollars on veterinary services restoring it to health, and christened it Gee Gee. Back in prime condition and serving as mascot, it lived in the storage yard, roamed the secret passageways of the historic warehouse (once a famous inn), and regularly kicked sections out of the yard fence to make social jaunts throughout the county, occasionally spending the night in jail. Which it did in Tarrytown, following which its owner decided to buy a moving van to simplify the recurrent task of bringing Gee Gee home.

When the mule, then a famous country character, finally met its demise as a parkway hit-and-run victim in the wee hours of a summer morning, its owner erected a monument to it in the form of a giant gilded-steel mule, a weathervane which has remained atop the headquarters of one of the country's major wreckers for more than a quarter century. But the firm is not without a mascot. A new mule, shipped anonymously to the wrecker's office, now roams the secret passageways, emerges mysteriously to greet customers (as it did our geologist friend in Chapter 1), and munches oats from a desk drawer in the office of the company president.

Often, too, it's the materials that have the dramatic background, like one tremendous load of used bricks in Chicago. They came from a major wrecking company that was called to the scene of a fire and explosion on North La Salle Street. It was a simple matter of knocking down teetering walls and clearing debris, but it turned up one of the incredible twists that every wrecker sometimes encounters and never forgets. Twelve hours after the big cranes rumbled onto the scene, tumbling and loading rubble, a workman suddenly flagged them to a stop. He had heard something, or thought he had, in the mountain of brick and cinders. Carefully, the cranes went back to work lifting the twisted girders like jackstraws. The man they unearthed recovered.

Sometimes it's a fortune instead of a life that's at stake. Such was the case when a famous wrecking firm rolled its fleet of trucks and machines out of the company's warehouse headquarters in a former Westchester County speakeasy to wreck a towering suburban apartment building. The wrecker, an old-timer in the business, had a strange feeling about this particular job, and called his office from the site to double-check every detail. But everything was in order. He watched his crew as they followed the starting routine of removing doors and windows from the top down. And he watched the big heating plants hoisted out of the basement. But when he saw a moving van move a family into the bottom of the building as his men were demolishing the top, he conveyed his strange feeling about the job to the real estate firm that had contracted for it.

A limousine screeching to a stop outside soon brought the answer. Somewhere in the real estate firm's business complex somebody goofed and ordered the wrong building torn down. It was the only time that wrecker was paid first to take a building apart, then put it back together, and finally to wreck the building that should have been wrecked in the first place.

If you have some used bricks in your patio or garden walk, think about this. If they don't have a story behind them, you can make up your own. Maybe you can adapt the incident you've just read to make your guests more interested in your bricks.

If You Want to Try It

Find your wrecker in your local yellow pages. If you want to buy materials for a whole house, buy them at the wrecking site itself. This minimizes the wrecker's costs and time, since he need not transport them to his wrecking yard. So you save. Building materials from a wrecker can be had at roughly half price compared to new, and have the advantage that they have been cut to sizes most often used in standard construction. The lumber is also end-squared and seasoned. Nails left in from the wrecking job can be pulled or driven in, whichever is easier.

If you're building, windows and doors are often a real bargain, especially as the hardware is usually still attached to the units, saving money and work, as when hinges are already in place.

Fixtures for bath and kitchen are worth

looking for at the wrecker's yard. (We bought all the fixtures for two bathrooms for less than the price of one new tub.) Ranges and refrigerators are comparable. We've bought automatic ranges at prices from $12 to $40, in top condition.

Also look for antiques and semi-antiques . . . furniture, china, and bric-a-brac. Ornate carvings on ugly old pieces can often be used on other pieces.

Usually, carvings on the otherwise unattractive furniture can be removed undamaged by soaking the carved area in a tub of water or by covering it with wet rags. (We bought an overly ornamental old fireplace front for $3 to get carvings that would have cost far more from a cabinetmaker's supply house.) An overnight wetting by either method usually softens the animal glue commonly used in old furniture. One decor-minded friend of ours simply left an old ornate bed out in his backyard for a few weeks and let the rain loosen the parts he wanted.

The water treatment comes in handy too if you have a valued piece of furniture that happens to have one of a pair of matched carvings missing, and a matching carving can't be bought. Simply remove the remaining carving and replace both of them with a pair taken from a piece of house wrecker's furniture. Naturally, pick something that comes as close to a match for the originals as possible. With a little ingenuity and wood filler, you can make it all come out right.

Garage doors of the overhead type are also among wrecker's bargains from time to time, as are home heating units of all the usual types. (You can often save 50 percent or more.) Things like this, however, require a little know-how, in order to check their condition and to install them. If you don't know anything about the thing you want to buy cheap, take somebody with you who knows, and also have him help you install it. Otherwise you may end up with a fiasco, and you can't blame the wrecker. In general, items like these are in reasonably good condition, as wreckers don't waste space storing things that aren't salable. But some repairs or replacement parts may be necessary, and you need to know what they are.

If you want something the wrecker doesn't have but is likely to have at another time, ask if you can arrange to have someone call you if the item comes in. (Some wreckers keep a calling and mailing list.) We got an almost new refrigerator this way at a saving of 80 percent, and one of our friends got enough solid teak paneling for his dining room at 10 cents a square foot. Another one bought a magnificent crystal chandelier for the price of an ordinary fixture. The man who wanted the cannonballs (mentioned earlier) got them by leaving word with a number of wreckers.

If you're looking for stuffed furniture, like the $2 chair in the photograph, you sometimes need to do some restoration work on it. But if you don't feel like fussing with broken-down springs and the traditional methods of making the thing shipshape (if it happens to be a little bedraggled but you still want it), think about tossing the old springs in the trash. You can usually replace the insides with foam rubber or one of the plastic foams used for the same purpose.

We did this with several chairs and a sofa simply by fastening quarter-inch plywood under the thing and up the back with screws, and letting the foam rest on the plywood. The new upholstery covers the whole works anyway. Just buy the foam thick enough and firm enough so you won't hit bottom with a klunk when you sit down. You can make a few trial sittings on the foam before you buy it. You simply staple the new upholstery on the same way as the old stuff. (On old furniture, it's usually held by hundreds of tacks. Don't stick your fingers with them.) We did

Wreckers store upholstered chairs indoors. This one cost $2. If you buy something like this at a price like this, don't tell the truth about it. People don't believe you. Lie about it. You can make people happy that way. See Chapter 11.

the job on our chairs and loveseat in an afternoon, and saved just about $400, compared to the going price at the time for the same combination at a furniture store. This amounts to working for almost $100 an hour, which isn't bad pay, as it adds up to nearly a quarter million a year. If you could only get your hands on the money you save this way. But you come out ahead, anyhow.

There are some things you won't find at a house wrecker's. Things like shingles and linoleum. These are among the materials that seldom can be removed undamaged from a building being razed. But the wrecking crew can unhitch almost everything else without making it unsalable. Anytime you have an opportunity to watch them work, do it. You'll learn some very useful tricks that will come in handy if you ever have to take anything apart—like a wall between two rooms that you'd like to remodel into one room.

If you learn that a particular building you're familiar with is about to be torn down, and there's anything in it you'd like to have, get your oar in quickly. Many a homeowner has acquired a nostalgic bit of treasure from such places as New York's old Waldorf and Ritz Carlton hotels and the old Metropolitan Opera House, and more recently, from Yan-

This chair, from a roof-high pile of chairs at a building wrecker's storage yard, was one of several dozen that sold for 50 cents apiece.

kee Stadium's remodeling job. If you wait too long before asking the price of what you want, a hundred other people may ask the same thing and push up the price.

From a practical standpoint, when you see a building being demolished, ask on the spot about the price of any materials you happen to need at the time. Buying at the wrecking site is almost always cheaper, even in small quantities. And don't forget things like the TV antenna and the doghouse on the back lawn. If it's a restaurant, maybe you'd like the bar. If it's a big one, you can cut it in sections to share with your neighbors. It's happened before. And have a look at any kitchen utensils that are still around. You may wind up with a pizza platter or two, or some oversized pots and pans for your next cookout. We have a pair of beautiful old cast-iron griddles we acquired that way for 50 cents apiece. But sometimes the wrecker won't sell. One of the few items not for sale at a major East Coast wrecker's headquarters are the two-foot-diameter frying pans that came from an old inn, and now play a major role once a year at the wrecking company's picnic and fish fry.

If You Can't Join It, Rent It

When the house you've been renting has been sold and you can't find anything else, you might as well have a drink where the atmosphere offers inspiration. We had in mind the beautiful Old Beagle Club in the hills of the wealthy Greenwich back country, one of our favorite spots in times of tempest. But we never got the drink. The place was closed, cold, and empty, with a frigid wind whistling through the leafless trees around it. Which, at an earlier date, we might have considered disheartening. But we had tasted the fruits of the Getting Game and had caught its theme of thinking big. What had once been a millionaire's estate, then a private club, and later a thriving inn should certainly be a nice place to live. So we came back the next day and stayed for seven years, renting one of the biggest estates in the town for less than the cost of a one-room apartment.

HOUSE IN SNOW
The ten-room house that went with our estate had
its own private bridge over the river and lots of other
things that made it a bargain rental for less than
a one-room apartment.

It was the first time we had a forty-foot living room, a
barroom, a whole floor of bedrooms, an outdoor dance
floor, a private lake, and our own bridge over a river. Plus
a couple of huge barns and something like 150 acres. But
we managed to become accustomed to it.

Of course, you can't just go out and find this sort of
bargain whenever you want to. You have to look for

45

places like that in the right areas, which we did by accident. And the situation has to be just right. It's a sometime thing, but we know people who have done it more than once. So it pays to know how to grab the brass ring when you see it.

Part of the explanation lies in the fact that lavish country homes are less of an insurance risk when they are occupied than when they are not. And if they happen to be part of a package priced in the hundreds of thousands of dollars, they just may not be sold overnight. Especially if they're tangled up in the legalities of wills and estates. So, at times, you can rent a castle on a clerk's income. And it's fun.

If you happen to see a big deserted mansion in the course of your daily travels, ask people in the area about it. The man in the gas station down the road, or in the nearest bar or liquor store. You'll get some fascinating tales, and eventually, the hard facts that may lead you to a bonanza, either for rent or for sale. But don't be surprised at anything. Some years later, when we were house hunting again, we just missed another bargain whose owner had died, gun in hand, in the course of a shootout with the police. And a few miles away, we could have bought a lovely little country church for about the price of a new car, if we had been more inquisitive. (Another house hunter bought it.)

If your budget isn't up to buying a house of peculiar background, it may be necessary to adjust to the possibility of having to live like a millionaire because the only thing you can rent at a fair price is a mansion—if you're lucky enough to find one in the proper circumstances. But make sure you won't have hotel-style running expenses. Our bargain estate had two heating systems, including a sixty-year-old coal-fired steam boiler, plus fireplaces everywhere. And the kitchen was equipped to feed a small army, which meant that anything smaller than a steamboat roast could get lost in the oven. So, to manage breakfast in time to catch the 8:12, my wife preferred to use a little camp stove in the west wing of the kitchen under the skylight.

When you take over something palatial, it is only natural that your neighbors take some notice as they drive by—you might be the advance echelon of some giant conglomerate about to open an executive office complex. If you happen to have a free Rolls-Royce parked in your courtyard, as we did, and a leaping, beer-drinking Irish water spaniel in plain sight, however, the tension is relieved. Conglomerates seldom are accompanied by Irish water spaniels.

One of the pleasant phenomena about the high style of doing things is learning how the other half lives. Millionaires who drive their own cars get stuck in the snow just like other people, for example. One of them thanked us profusely for lending him a shovel when he bogged down right in front of our private bridge. And when the next blizzard arrived he sailed up our private road in the most luxurious snow plow money could buy, and plowed us out. On his way to the train. Which saved the day for us, as we had to catch the same train and couldn't afford snow tires for our Rolls-Royce.

If You Want to Try It

Look for lavish vacant estates in high-priced areas. Resort spots are a good bet for seasonal bargain rentals . . . out of season, of course, but comfortable, sometimes furnished. A great way to spend the time between an expired lease on your old digs and the finishing of a new home, or to use as a pied-à-terre while real estate hunting. If you are willing to take on some caretaking, you have a wider year-round choice. Just be sure you don't take on a burden you can't cope with.

The best candidates for unbelievable rentals are likely to be impressively large but empty homes from a past era, surrounded by extensive grounds that appear neglected. Tall grass and weeds waving in the wind are a good sign. Peeling paint here and there on the house is also encouraging.

When you inquire of other residents in the area, you may not always meet the resident himself. It may be the butler or gardener.

Simply say you have been looking for a house like the vacant one ever since you gave up your place in the Bahamas, and would like to locate the proper person to contact about it. This way, nobody will suspect the truth about you, and you are more likely to get the information you want.

Often, you will be told the place is tied up in an estate and can't be sold at the present time, which is frequently the truth. But somewhere along the line you are likely to find somebody in the picture who would like to have a tenant living in it for practical reasons. For one, an occupied house is less likely to suffer from vandalism than an empty one. And there may also be a saving on insurance.

If you happen to get a warm response to your efforts from the powers behind the house (a bank may be involved), arrange to look it over inside before you jump at it. Our lucky find had two heating systems, both of which worked after some minor attention. If something important is missing, like the furnace, however, you won't want to replace it yourself. And thieves have been known to strip long-vacant houses of just about everything from plumbing to heating. In more than one case, they have stolen the entire house, though usually not an enormous one.

Once you move in (assuming you can manage a deal), there are certain things you should forget about. Forget about anything that requires work on very old steel water pipes, for example, even though you have the blessing of the owners of the house to make some improvements. We know of one instance where the joyful tenant of a bargain-rate old mansion hired a plumber to install a new water heater. This would have been an inexpensive job if the ancient pipes hadn't crumbled everywhere the plumber tried to disconnect them with a wrench. As it finally cost more than three times as much as the heater, figure that you'll be better off with moderately warm water or even tepid water until you pick a sweepstakes winner.

Of course, if you're lucky enough to make one of these bargain mansion deals, you may also be lucky enough to find everything shipshape. Ours didn't have much wrong. But we found it pays to explore the whole place thoroughly. In the first big town house we ever rented for a song (before the country estate with the two hundred acres), we noticed some interesting things among the ashes in two of the fireplaces. Like antique cabinet locks and handwrought hardware. In the course of exploring the cellar, we found a big woodbin that provided the explanation in the form of a collection of beautiful furniture that had been chopped to pieces. While this is probably not a common occurrence, keep in mind that with modern glue you can probably reassemble chopped-up furniture, in case you have an experience like that. We found all the pieces of lots of of things, including a charming pair of end tables. And, on shelves near the coal-fired steam boiler, we located the insides of a player piano—nice shiny machinery that apparently stayed behind when the piano was chopped up for firewood.

In the beautiful big place with all the acreage, the only real flaw we found was a missing skylight in the attic, which accounted for the interesting coloration of the bedroom ceilings on the floor below. The skylight turned up in the tulip garden near the outside dance floor, and we locked it back in place with no difficulty—except for a little bedroom redecorating, which we would probably have done anyway.

While you are in the process of making your mansion livable, you can expect frequent interruptions by salesmen, who have an uncanny way of spotting new signs of life in an old place. If they aim to sell you things you don't want, you simply say the owner is spending the season on the Riviera, and you are just the cleaning man, and you work by the day. (Your wife can say she's the temporary upstairs maid.) If anybody wants to demonstrate something like a vacuum cleaner, you, as the butler, can permit the demonstration, which may save you some cleaning work, but must stipulate you can only make recommendations to the owners of the house when they get back from the Riviera.

If word gets around that the house is being prepared by a butler and a maid, however, you may have to ward off wealthy neighbors who would like to hire you. If so, you can always say you've been with the family for years and wouldn't care to change unless the pay was substantially higher than the yearly $35,000 you have been getting. This should not only serve as a stopper, but make it apparent that the new owner is either a billionaire or a nut. And, of course, if it doesn't serve as a stopper, maybe, at such a price, you'd like to be a butler.

If the place you rent happens to have been a club or an inn, as in the case of our country estate, you can expect to meet many genial people with puzzled expressions on their faces. It usually happens just as you sit down to dinner. You answer a knock at the door, and a

group of smiling men and women parade
into your living room and ask what you have
done with the bar, because they want a few
drinks before dinner, and also what the hell
became of all the tables. The simplest solu-
tion is to tell them the truth. But if you happen to be wearing white tie and tails and are
ready to leave for a grand ball, they may
not believe you, because you look like the
maître d'.

We had that happen during our first
month in the place, and it was very apparent
that one of the cigar-puffing would-be guests
we turned away thought I was just a greedy
headwaiter saving space for the big tippers.
We saw him again the following New Year's
Eve while we were waiting for a table we
had reserved at our favorite night spot. And
he was still so sure I was a greedy headwaiter that he demanded I show him and his
party to their table immediately. He was not
going to stand around like a damn fool, he
said, and if I planned to keep him waiting
while other people got all the tables, he might
just pick me up by the scruff of my neck
and throw me the hell out of the place, because people like me should be kicked out of
the restaurant business anyway.

Since I couldn't seem to reach him with
the fact that I wasn't the headwaiter, I made

peace by escorting him and his group to the biggest table with a reserved sign on it. And to placate him I suggested a first course of french-fried caviar, which I said was only for special guests because of the limited supply. If he was not served promptly, all he had to do was let me know, I said. Just ask for Garibaldi.

From where we sat we could see waiters bringing drinks to him and his friends, and everything seemed to be going smoothly until the people who had reserved the big table arrived and were guided to it by the headwaiter. We could just hear snatches of what was said at that point, but there was a highly accented argument regarding just who Garibaldi was and where in hell he expected to find french-fried caviar.

Later we saw the restaurateur himself mopping his brow and saying he wished he had become a violinist like his father had hoped. By that time everybody was wearing colorful New Year's party hats, which fortunately made me look less like a headwaiter, so we weren't afraid to dance. Even though the man with the cigar might still be looking for Garibaldi.

Steinway in the Snow

Almost anybody will tell you that you can't buy a Steinway grand piano for $20. At least, not one that you can expect to play. But that is not necessarily so. The $4,000 Steinway grand we've been playing for years cost us exactly $20, and we still have the receipt for it. If you're alert, self-confident, and open-minded, there's a fair chance you can get one the same way. Quite a few people have. The procedure is likely to be a little harrowing at some points, but it's all over in a few days and you save thousands of dollars and end up with a magnificent musical instrument. Just how much of an adventure it is depends on the individual circumstances, but ours was probably typical, even if some of the reasons behind it were not.

At the time, we were renting a two-hundred-acre estate in the posh Greenwich back country in order to keep our expenses at a minimum, as explained in Chapter 4. But we had learned that big luxurious homes require lots of big luxurious furniture, and look very empty without it. In fact, we used up our handful of furniture so early in the game that our forty-foot living room had nothing in it but a sofa and a couple of rolling bars, which tended to create the atmosphere of a deserted saloon.

So we naturally got to thinking about the kind of furniture we'd rather have. For a touch of elegance, we figured that a grand piano, which we had always wanted anyway, would be just right. But our budget for such nonessentials between any two paydays at the time was around $20, which doesn't get you a grand piano by normal methods. And our building-demolishing friends (from Chapter 2) had nothing but uprights.

We visited piano dealers anyway, just to check on rock-bottom prices, and looking back on it, we probably created the wrong image in their minds. When we pulled up to a showroom in our Rolls-Royce and then asked to see the cheapest secondhand grand in the place, they undoubtedly decided we were like a lot of other wealthy tightwads. And when we mentioned that our top limit was $20 they laughed, because it's good policy to laugh at a customer's jokes. Then they showed us bargains we could have for as little as a thousand dollars. Rumpus-room pianos, they sometimes called them. The kind of "second" pianos you don't worry about when you throw a party.

All in all, we simply didn't get through to them. And it

was probably just as well. The way we looked at it, if you can get a Rolls-Royce without spending a cent, $20 should certainly be enough to pay for a mere grand piano. Even if other people are willing to spend thousands. All we had to do was find the right source.

Companies that rebuild pianos, we decided, might be the answer. And, as I had recently walked right by one of these when I got off at the wrong subway stop, that place could be a starting point. Maybe they'd like to sell some kind of a grand cheap before they rebuilt it. After all, we figured, if they could rebuild it, so could we, which is the kind of confidence you definitely must have for this type of bargain hunting. Besides, we once had an old upright with a lot of keys that didn't work, and we made them work just by tying some parts together. No trouble at all once we looked inside. All we needed was a ball of string to replace some little pieces of tape the mice had gnawed loose, and everything was fine. So an un-rebuilt wreck made sense.

The white-haired German foreman who guided us through the piano-rebuilding plant was proud to show us his skilled gnomes at work on pianos in various stages of rehabilitation. "Oldt pianos never die," he told us. But also, none ever left his establishment until they were completely rebuilt. And his gnomes could rebuild them no matter what had happened to them, so long as the plate wasn't broken, the plate being the big iron frame inside. After all, as he explained it, buying a damaged piano would be silly when for a mere thousand dollars or so we could have it completely rebuilt. Which, had we been fainthearted, might have ended our bargain hunt once and for all. We already knew from nights of scanning the newspapers that we wouldn't find a $20 grand piano in the classified ads. But what we didn't know was that we might find one in the headlines. If we knew what to look for. And that's the trick.

It was our friend who drove the police patrol car who first called our attention to this possibility in connection with a very distinctive Steinway he thought might be priced within our budget. Of course, after what was in the paper, he cautioned us that other people might be interested in it. But fortunately, he said, practically everybody, including the millionaire who owned the piano, had been afraid to go near it for several days because of the situation in the music room where the piano was located. So, if we acted quickly, we might be the first to make an offer.

All we had to do was look it over and decide whether we wanted to make a deal on the price. If so, our police friend was sure he could find some piano movers with the know-how and the nerve to go into the music room and bring the thing out.

The only problem was in the condition of the millionaire's home. As the newspapers had reported, one wing of it had burned almost to the ground, but the music room was still standing. And the ceiling had fallen on top of the piano, which happened to have its lid open at the time. The fire hoses had filled it with sooty water and charred fragments of various things, all of which had frozen over and now lay covered with a foot of snow. So the piano was likely to require some attention.

When we went to see it, one of the dealers we had met was working his way out of a hole in the music-room wall, as the floor in front of the doorway had dropped into the cellar. He smiled politely and looked at us appraisingly as we stood there beside our Rolls-Royce holding our ax and bucket. Then he drove away.

As the weather had turned warmer, the last of the water was running out of the piano and we didn't need our bailing bucket. We just used our ax to chop the remaining ice into chunks we could lift out so we could see inside. From looking at new pianos we had a rough idea of what the inside should look like, and, of course, we wanted to see the iron frame we had been told was so important. We learned, however, that you can't see much by shining a dim flashlight into a soot-coated piano. But since it hadn't fallen through the floor, we decided the frame wasn't broken. And as the rest of its innards, though black and soggy, were still discernible, we concluded it was definitely the piano for us. If the price was right. (Admittedly, it is possible to base your piano-buying decisions on more substantial evidence. But when you're buying a Steinway grand for the price of a pair of shoes, cut loose and gamble a little.)

Not surprisingly, the owner thought it odd that any-body would want a piano that had been declared a total loss by experts that very morning, so I explained that it was to be used merely as a background in a photo studio. Which in a way was true, since I eventually took the pic-ture of it on page 67. (So as not to raise doubts as to your mental condition, it is wise to have a logical explanation in this kind of situation.)

Of course, not all fire-sale pianos are full of water. Many are merely roasted, not steamed. The trick is in finding one that is just short of hopeless and such a ter-rible mess that you could buy a new one for the cost of having it fixed up professionally. Then nobody, including the insurance people, want it. And you can name your own price, which in our case was the $20 that closed the deal. (If you're really cheap, try $5.)

Late that afternoon the hardy movers who had laid timbers across the hole in the floor delivered the piano to our living room, where it stood dripping black juice on the floor. And the log fires we hoped would help dry the thing crackled cheerily in both fireplaces. Yet there was something unnerving in realizing we were now the out-right owners of a big wet grand piano that experts had branded a worthless wreck. (Prepare yourself for this with a drink.)

One of the movers commented that the keys looked like potato chips, and we acknowledged that we could use a batch of new ivories. Somebody also mentioned having seen an old upright lying on its back in a barn some-place with stray cats living in it, and suggested it as a possible source of keys. Then the movers left as quickly as they had come, and we were alone with our Steinway. This is the moment of truth when the show really begins and you are on your own.

You discover things about your prize that you didn't notice before. Under the light of the room's main crystal chandelier, we found that the things we had fixed so easily in the old upright were out of reach under the rusty steel strings of the grand. And many of them were in dire need beneath scorched debris and great globs of soggy plaster. In this situation, if you have an average circle of friends, you realize you don't know anybody who can tell you how to take a grand piano apart. Most people simply go through life without doing it.

Actually, however, the chances are you do know some-body who has done it, and who will tell you how. In our case it was Herman, the weekend pianist at one of our favorite bistros. (We have found since that many dealers will tell you how, but Herman did much more to lift our spirits. Keep this in mind, as morale is vital to this type of work.)

From this stage on, whether you get your guidance from a bistro pianist, a dealer, or this book, you're likely to be more of a repairman than an adventurer. In any event, your work will progress more pleasantly if you can combine the initial steps with some sort of party, which also provides helping hands.

For example, it was over a few bourbons from one of our rolling bars that we gave Herman the details of our fire-sale bargain. Then he did something that we would have sworn was impossible if we hadn't seen him do it. In just thirty seconds he took the front off the Steinway and pulled out the entire works, including the keys and all the machinery that goes with them, and laid it on the bar like a tray of hors d'oeuvres. "You call that bunch of stuff the action," he said.

Then he put it all back together again just as quickly as he took it apart, and said, "Now you do it."

Having seen him do it, even though it was hard to believe, we took it apart almost as fast as he did. Since you'll probably have to do it too, if you acquire a broken-down grand, you should know how it's done.

The first thing to do is look at a grand piano from the front. Almost all grand pianos have a narrow wooden strip (finished like the rest of the piano) overlapping the front ends of the keys at the bottom, the way your lower lip overlaps your lower teeth. Piano people call this the key slip. On most grands all you have to do is lift this thing up and it comes off. If it sticks, you can try prying up the ends gently with a nail file or a butter knife.

Once the key slip is off, you can see the space under the keys, and also the front end of a block at each end of the keyboard. The blocks lift up and off, along with the lid that covers the keys. You have to tilt the lid, which piano people call the fall board, so that it clears the other parts on the way out. Then you simply slide out the works, and don't drop it. Also, if the piano is a real mess, flip the front of the top lid back before you slide the thing out, to make sure none of the felt hammers is in the up position, where it can hook on to something and break on the way out. Once the action is out, you can fix it up your own way, as explained shortly, but don't mention your methods to any piano people, or you'll probably upset them.

We didn't put the piano back together directly after taking it apart because there were things to fix, and also there was a lot of knocking at the front door. Which turned out to be a tall man with a paper bag full of piano keys. "Nate says somebody here wants piano keys," he said jovially. "So I took 'em off the old piano out in the barn—gives the cats a little more room."

He accepted our invitation to join the festivities, just for a quickie, and Herman, after spreading the keys out on the rug, asked for a flatiron—or preferably, two flatirons—and some wet rags. What he did with them you'll want to know if your piano also has keys that look like potato chips.

In short, he laid a cluster of the newly arrived keys close together with a wet rag on top, and placed the flatiron, moderately hot, on top of the rag, which hissed out a little steam. A minute or so later, after the heat had softened the glue, he pried off ivories with his penknife. Then he removed the potato-chip ivories the same way, and used some of our white glue to replace them with the good ones, which, happily, were the same size. (The width doesn't vary much, but the length of the ivory pieces isn't always the same. This is important if you buy them new, which you can usually do—from a piano dealer.)

Meanwhile my wife used cellulose cement to stick some of the felt hammers back together where they had popped apart from their steam bath, and tied them with silk thread. And somebody was knocking on a door somewhere. At the same time, as the room was very hot from the two fireplaces and I had set up another round from the bar, Herman began to sing *Trink, Trink, Brüderlein, Trink!,* which had a very nice lilt to it. Then I noticed several of our neighbors had dropped in through the back door and were sitting on the floor at the other end of the room drinking highballs and sorting piano keys.

Our little afternoon piano party ran well into the night, with steaks charcoaled in one of the fireplaces and Herman actually playing the piano, which had finally stopped dripping.

The important point in all of this is that once we found out how to get the thing apart, we were able to fix most of what needed fixing, all in one night. And, with the possible exception of Herman, with clearly unskilled labor. Which means that just about anybody can do it. Herman told us, however, that not all makes are as easy to take apart as a Steinway. For some you need a screwdriver, and you have to look for screws to take out.

Also on Herman's advice, we allowed a couple of weeks

PIANO
After the Steinway was restored during several cocktail affairs we refinished it and had it tuned.

for drying time before we called a piano tuner. We used
that time for scraping off the char, filling rough spots,
and finishing the piano in much the same way we had
finished our $39 sloop (page 86). Except that we used
low-sheen black enamel on the piano to approximate
what piano makers usually call an ebony finish. This,
unlike glossy paint, hides bumps and other evidence of

blundering, and it's available just about everywhere. In between paint jobs, the piano can be played. You can swab the sooty film from the brightwork inside the piano with detergent on everything from wrung-out sponges to Q-Tips, and use the wet rag and flatiron stunt to flatten down the veneer ripples found on most fire-roasted piano tops. You just move the iron along the ripple slowly to soften the glue and restick it, while somebody else slides a tray of ice cubes right behind the iron to chill the glue before the ripple pops up again. You can use the ice cubes later for their usual purpose. The rest of the job is just a matter of patience and sandpaper, preferably aluminum oxide, starting with medium grit and ending with fine.

When our tuner finally came, he looked at the serial number on the big iron frame and said the piano had been made before he was born and that it was the exact model one of his customers wanted if he could get it for a thousand or so. (The customer offered us $900 later in the week.)

We mentioned that we had replaced the ivories on most of the keys, and he complimented us. It was the kind of thing you can do yourself if you're careful, he said. You can even learn to tune a piano if you have a good ear. "But *never, never* touch the action!"

Which gives some indication of the difference in the way the pros and the non-pros look at the subject. If you want to get a piano this way, you need a little reckless daring.

When a mansion or restaurant fire hits the headlines, look into the piano possibilities—but, with tact. If you saunter up to a man who is surveying the wreckage of his business or the family homestead and ask him how much he wants for his grand piano, he may respond with a shower of tears or a hard right to the jaw. Which could spoil your whole day.

The local paper, the police, the fire department, and local insurance companies are possible sources of information. From there on you have to play it by ear. Insurance people are especially accustomed to remaining businesslike under disaster conditions. As are workmen who often appear on the scene shortly after a disaster.

About a month after the fire that produced our bargain, we spoke to one of the workmen who was rebuilding the place. We asked him how things were going with the job, and he told us everything was coming along hotsy dandy. But he said we should have seen it the day after the place burned down, when he was first called to size up the job. There were thousands of dollars' worth of fancy furniture in the place, he said. A big, burned-up grand piano full of water with the ceiling on top of it, and velvet upholstered chairs and inlaid cabinets, and all kinds of beautiful stuff. Then poof! it's all burned up.

I said it's a crazy world, and he agreed. "Crazier than you think," he said. "Some nut bought the piano."

If You Want to Try It

Newspaper accounts of fires in restaurants and mansions are a good beginning for a search like this. Get to the scene of the disaster as soon as possible and discover all you can about the situation, especially the insurance people involved. It is to everyone's advantage to dispose of damaged furnishings and appliances promptly. The price depends on their condition. If the price is right, buy on the spot. If you don't, somebody else will.

The Car on
the Barroom Floor

Some things you simply can't buy ready-made even if you're willing to spend money. For example, you can't just walk into a showroom and buy a twenty-foot canary-yellow convertible with mahogany trim, a disappearing kitchen, two beer coolers, a bar, a freight compartment, and air conditioning. Plus a radio, tape player, hot and cold running water, sleeping accommodations, and a total weight of three tons. But you can think about it. And if you're downright determined, you can probably build it. Maybe even in your house, if you have an empty barroom.

When we did it we were influenced by a number of things, including the fact that we didn't like to carry greasy outboard motors in the back of our Rolls-Royce when we had a good chance of selling it for a tidy profit. And, of course, we liked the idea of a big luxurious car if it didn't cost much. Say, not more than $500.

This three-ton giant was a traffic stopper. It was built in our bar, and was equipped with bar and kitchen, two beer coolers, a radio, heater, and tape player (when they didn't have tape players). It would reach 105 mph.

Naturally, when you discuss this sort of thing with people you are apt to hear discouraging comments like how tremendous manufacturers with whole teams of engineers have to spend millions of dollars just to develop an ordinary car. And even then they may have to recall millions of them because something doesn't work.

But actually, building your own car isn't as difficult as it sounds if you make the business end of it by combining parts of other cars that somebody else has already figured out. But you may have to do things that upset you, to get the combination you need. We had to hacksaw the back end of the body of an enormous old Cadillac so we could get at the rusty bolts that held the rest of it on. If you have never sawed the body off a Cadillac you may find it disturbing, as may others who watch you. One of our neighbors who had greatly admired the Cadillac when we drove it home the preceding day, became extremely emotional when he saw us expedite the body removal with a fire ax, and didn't speak to us again until the following summer.

Once you have passed the demolition phase, however, spectators are likely to regard you merely as an eccentric rather than a madman. And the work itself is more pleasant.

The nature of the car body, of course, is up to you. Since you are building it, you can make it any size and shape you want, and pick your own materials. We used sheet aluminum over an oak framework because aluminum and wood are easy to work with, and the whole thing could be moved around on little furniture dollies. You can get the wood from any lumberyard, and find somebody who sells aluminum in your classified phone book. And you can find the other essentials, like the mechanisms that crank up the windows, in any junkyard.

As we started our custom car job in the fall, we simply parked the chassis in the barn (you can use a garage) and built the body in the house, where it was more comfortable. We found too that the seats, when properly braced, made nice little sofas, which we needed for parties in the section of the house that had once been the club's barroom. And as we had already marked the outline of the car on the barroom floor, it was very easy to slide the little sofas into position whenever we were mapping out the other components of the car, like the bar, and the folding kitchen, and the beer coolers.

Even when we began to build the body itself, the seats served as party sofas, as all you had to do was open one of the car doors and get into the seat. In fact, after the bar and beer coolers were installed the rear sofa was the most popular seat in the house, and the front sofa with the tape player a close second. Naturally, too, if you use an automobile body as furniture it becomes something of a conversation piece.

Be sure that any automobile body you build in your house will fit through the doors, so you can get it out. Fortunately, our barroom had extra-wide French doors that gave us leeway. And we didn't mount the convertible top until the body was bolted to the chassis. If your wife is very skilled and very enthusiastic, she can probably make the top, after watching a professional. That's how we got ours, and it was perfect, as the photo shows. Otherwise go to a top-maker.

In the course of your car building, don't treat the instrument panel lightly. Follow the lead of the big-

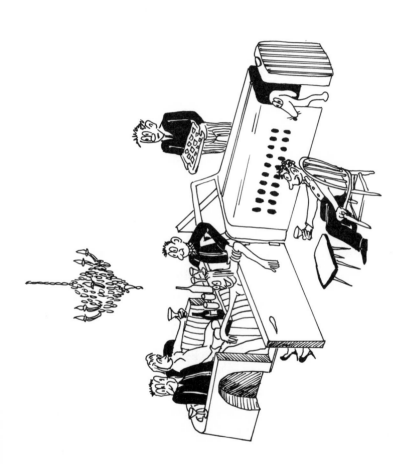

timers and make this a focal point of the car. It should have an impressive array of instruments, including the ones you need, or idiot lights if they were the original equipment. Whether the rest of the instruments do anything or not is immaterial, so long as they look interesting and cover all available space. For only $3 we bought a useless but fascinating group from an old wrecked airplane that a Connecticut house wrecker kept on the roof of his headquarters for display. Dime-store dial thermometers also add a touch. If anyone is rude enough to ask why any of them seem inactive, simply say they monitor the car's auxiliary systems, which normally are inoperative.

Along with the body, by all means build a new hood and radiator shell to give your car a unique foreign look. This not only makes it distinctive, but practically theft-proof. We topped off our radiator shell with a beautiful name plate from a Zeiss-Ikon camera display contributed by a friend who ran a photo shop. You can also get beautiful emblems from liquor-store displays. If anyone comments that he never knew Michelob build automobiles, tell them that's how the company started, just like Budweiser and Offenhauser. We always said ours was from the Zeiss Motor Division that built the famous F-22 wide-angle fighter planes.

And by all means, paint your custom car a bright color and use something like mahogany for trim. You can cut the mahogany wide enough to cover any wavy seams in your bodywork, which are likely unless you happen to run a body shop. As doors take time to make, we made our car a two-door, with doors five feet long, which even General Motors couldn't match.

The climax of it all is, of course, the maiden voyage, which may turn up certain minor malfunctions. As mentioned in Chapter 1, our air-conditioning system, which was made from the innards of an old butcher-shop refrigerator, actually overperformed. And, because of the extremely hot and humid August weather, it prompted people to ask us why we had to scrape the frost from our windshield whenever we stopped for a traffic light, which was understandable.

The stream of smoke coming from under the backing light on the car's trunk was merely the flow from the broiler's exhaust fan, which is normal if you like your steaks seared. But it attracted a small crowd when we stopped at a liquor store. Some passersby also expressed concern at the little streams of water running out of the body behind the rear wheels. Until we explained that it was just draining from the ice in the beer coolers a little faster than it usually would because both cases of beer were fairly warm when they went in.

The only real oversight the maiden voyage revealed was in the eight-foot fenders, which lifted high above the hood when we encountered a headwind coming in from Long Island Sound, out on Steamboat Road. We corrected that just by inserting a couple of missing bolts that I still had in my jacket pocket.

From the first run on, however, you discover new advantages in a custom car, if it's strange enough. For one, you never have a problem finding it in a supermarket parking space, even if you can't remember where you left it. It simply stands out, and there's usually a cluster of people around it. So be sure to provide hood locks to protect the engine from the curious. If you stencil bold-face CAUTION signs on both sides of the hood the way we did, you can also save yourself from hot-rodding road-house attendants who insist on parking your car. "Too dangerous," you tell them, pointing to the sign. "The other one blew up in Detroit last month."

Then you park it yourself.

If You Want to Try It

You need a really good reason to build your own luxury car. If you like to eat, you might like to have a kitchen aboard, and maybe a bar to help you work up an appetite. Or, if you live in a cold winter area, you might like a car you can drive home from the station on blustery nights without having to spend half an hour scraping snow and ice off a sloping windshield and windows. Those were a few of the reasons we had for building our own luxury car. But whatever inspires you to such an effort, plan on it from the beginning. And try some small-scale wood and sheet-metal work for practice before you begin the big job.

You don't have to start with a big chassis, but it helps. For what we wanted, we needed the biggest one we could find that was in fair mechanical shape but with a nice rotten body to keep the price down. It's usually not hard to find one of these with rust holes all over it, terrible paint, dents, and ripped upholstery. (Maybe you already have one.) But if you're buying the thing, put it on a lift to be sure the frame and running gear haven't been knocked out of whack in a wreck.

The worse the body is, the easier it is to knock off. If it's bad enough, you can get at the bolts that hold it to the chassis simply by banging holes in it with a pickax. But save the instrument panel, the mechanisms that raise and lower the windows, and the door handles and latch units. You'll use them in the new body.

Best bet for the original car (unless it happens to be your own) is a used-car dealer, so you can give your prize a test run. If you have the patience, you can also do an overhaul on it the way we did. Once you've knocked the body off, it's a lot easier to get at everything.

We used aluminum over a hardwood frame for the body. In the old days when most car bodies had wood framework, the wood was usually ash. But oak is just as good (it's a little heavier) and you can get it at most lumberyards. Ours was cut from full inch (not nominal inch) white oak six and eight inches wide.

If you build the body in bridge-truss style, with diagonals wherever they won't get in the way of something like a window mechanism or a swing-away cookstove, it will have good rigidity and squeak resistance. (You don't want squeaks in a luxury car.) It's nice to know, too, that it has a fair chance of hanging together if you manage to roll it over.

After you have the chassis, but before you begin the body job, make a scale model of the car using heavy paper and balsa-wood framing, the way kids make model airplanes. Any curve you can form with the paper, you can form with the sheet aluminum without hammering to shape. Unless you have body-shop experience and the tools to go with it, avoid "compound" curves (like part of a ball) that require hammer shaping, and stick to "developable" curves (like a rolled piece of paper) that can be formed without hammering. This makes the job easier anyway, even if you have body-shop experience and tools. And it assures an offbeat appearance. (If you build something wild, it should look wild. We found this adds to the fun of the car.)

Avoid driving nails or screws through the aluminum to hold it to the frame unless you plan to conceal them with molding. And, of course, use molding to cover wavy seams or anything else you bungle a little. You can buy soft aluminum molding in assorted shapes that can be bent around almost any curve. (Get them where you get your sheet aluminum.) But you can usually cover more for less money with wood, like the mahogany we used, where the molding doesn't have to take a sharp curve. And the result is more spectacular.

You buy the aluminum in flat sheets from a metal distributor (look in your yellow pages), whose stock will consist of an assortment of numbered alloys, each suited to certain purposes. Number 6061 is a close match to the alloy we used. (The numbering system has been changed since then.) Pick the sheet sizes that will give you the most car body with the least waste (48-by-144-inch sheets worked out nicely for us). Tell your supplier what you want the aluminum for, and ask for a catalog. You may get some good ideas from both. The thickness we used was 16 gauge, which is about equal to $\frac{1}{20}$ inch.

Be sure the base of your body framework

can be bolted to the chassis at all points where the original body was bolted. And reinforce all framework joints with metal corner angles, reinforced where possible with resorcinol resin glue. (You can get the glue at most hardware stores.) Except for these specifics, your custom body can take just about any form you like. But plan your windows and windshield around available glass and windshield sizes. For a curved windshield (if you want one), your best bet is an auto junkyard. For flat shatterproof glass windows, have a glass dealer cut to the size you want, with edges polished.

If your wild ideas include a sofa for the front or back seat, check with your state motor vehicle department on the maximum permissible width of cars in your state. To make sure ours would get by in any state, we measured the width of a Cadillac, which at the time was eighty inches wide in that particular model. So, since we figured Cadillacs must be permitted in all states, we held our width to eighty inches.

If the finished job has any bumps or gaps in the surface when you get through with it, you can cover them with fiberglass cloth after leveling them with resin filler. (You can buy resin filler from auto supply dealers. You use polyester resin to stick on the fiberglass.) When you feather out the edges of the touch-ups with a sanding disk on your power drill, the whole patched area should be just about invisible after it's painted. Plenty of non-pro boat and car owners do this success-fully. (Even if you never build a luxury car, you may want to use this method on the family car if you bang it up. We covered five rust holes this way in our station wagon so well that we can't find them to brag about. For small jobs you can buy a fiberglass and resin kit from auto supply dealers.)

To avoid a wavy appearance in large body areas, plan your car so as to avoid completely flat surfaces. A slight curvature assures a smooth look and minimizes the chance of drumming noises from normal vibration.

To get a perfectly straight square corner, bend in the sheet metal, which you'll need at window and door openings, clamp the metal between lengths of fairly heavy angle iron (from any ironworking shop), and bend the protruding portion by hammering a hard-wood block against it. (This is another method that comes in handy even if you don't build yourself a car.) You can cut the metal with metal shears. Or, for a perfectly flat cut edge, you can use a saber saw with a metal-cutting blade.

For the final paint job we used auto lacquer over an aluminum primer, sold for the purpose. Check with the lacquer supplier on aluminum-surface preparation. We gave ours a wash with white vinegar, followed by a water rinse before the primer went on, and never had any paint problem. But ask questions when you buy your lacquer.

Be sure, of course, that your car has all the required equipment such as lights and safety belts, and be sure the belts won't let go. You can have the car weighed at a building supply dealer's where trucks are weighed out on a drive-on scale.

Before you decide on a built-in bar, check with your state motor vehicle department. There could be complications. But if you want to include a refrigerator and culinary equipment, as we did, you should face no liquor problem even in a dry state. Just remember not to flame your crêpe suzettes with cognac.

The White Monster

There are many good reasons for owning a roomy cabin sailboat. For one, it can serve as summer resort and beach club where you never have to reserve a room, tip a bellboy, or pay dues. And, of course, you don't have to buy gas or oil for it, and people don't expect you to tow them around on water skis.

Our problem, however, was the price of cabin sailboats. The kind we wanted cost too much, even secondhand. So if we wanted one, we'd have to build it, which a Southern friend of ours told us just about everybody did down where he came from. "It's just as easy as building a window box," he said. "Only it's bigger."

And, as things turned out, he wasn't far off. So long as you have the nerve. And it actually doesn't take much nerve to build a sailboat without knowing how and to sail

BOAT

The *Flying Smelt* was a very beamy boat which helped a lot when we went sailing in a gale—before we gave much thought to things like gales.

it without knowing how, if you don't know you don't know how. But you need some rules of thumb and a fair amount of luck.

Then, if your boat doesn't leak or sink, and if it sails beautifully for the next fifteen years until you sell it for ten times what it cost you to build it, you can figure you probably knew how in the first place. Which was how it worked out with our cabin sloop, the *Flying Smelt*.

The name, which we selected to distinguish our boat from the thousands named after big disagreeable fish like the barracuda, was just one of the things that set us apart from the yachting purists. Another was the economics of the thing. The *Flying Smelt* cost us just $39, complete with a two-burner stove, icebox and running water in the galley, a bar, all the amenities, and sleeping accommodations for four, plus a set of secondhand sails that carried our own handmade emblem of a big grinning face with one tooth. All of which made it something of an outcast in a field where people spend much more than that just for a steering wheel. (The *Flying Smelt* would cost about $300 today, still a major bargain.)

At least it was an outcast in the eyes of the traditional yachtsman. But dedicated sailing people like that have their own way of looking at things, and even speak a language of their own which they consider essential, although it can be very confusing to an outsider. Words like "heel" and "sole," for example, are so mixed up that the heel of a boat is how far it's tipped in the wind, and the sole is the floor of the cabin. And if a yachtsman tells you he has just put a shackle in the "head," he may mean he has hooked it to the top of the sail or dropped it in the toilet, which can make a big difference even though both things have the same name on a boat.

So, at the planning stage, we simply forgot about the language barrier, and whenever we ran across people who might have helpful knowledge, we asked elementary questions. Like what kind of wood was best for planking. The lumberyard people said that white pine, of which they had a tremendous supply, was just great. But our boating friends said that was absolutely wrong, and suggested everything expensive from imported mahogany to oak. So we compromised and decided to hang the rudder on a two-foot piece of oak and plank the rest of the boat with white pine because, at the time, it was the cheapest thing we could get. That's important if you're building a boat because you can't afford to buy one. (Eventually our compromise was interesting too, as the two-foot piece of oak was the only thing the worms ever ate. Even now when we mention this around boating people, somebody gets furious.)

People are very opinionated about things like this, so don't be discouraged if you get into a state of utter confusion during the information-gathering stage. (Today white pine is far from cheap anyway, and plywood makes things a lot easier.) Just keep reminding yourself that building a boat without experience is much less thrilling than sailing it without experience, which you'll eventually do. More about this later.

As to building know-how, just as you can learn to scramble eggs by watching a short-order cook, you can learn a lot about boat building by watching somebody else do it, as we did in a little one-man rowboat factory in Port Chester, New York. If you can't find a rowboat factory, you can still find out a lot by looking at the insides of boats in boatyards or tied up at docks. And, of course, there are boat-building books in the library that you can look at if you know when to shut your mind to what you see—such as complicated formulas and drawings that might stifle your self-expression, or even turn you off completely.

We simply made up *Flying Smelt* as we went along, like the Indians their canoes, and also like our Southern friend. Down where he lived, he said, when a man wanted to build a boat, he decided how long it was going to be according to the length of the side planks he could get, and then made a frame as wide as he wanted the middle of the boat to be. After that he just bent the planks around the frame and tied the ends together with rope so the boat would have a point at each end. Then he nailed a wedge-shaped piece called a stem inside each end so he could take the ropes off. "Nail a few more frames inside the thing, plank up the bottom, slap on some paint, and you got yourself a boat," he said. "Takes a couple days."

Of course, the boys along the river had their own ideas

and didn't do everything the same way. Like some of them who cut the sides so the bottom would curve up a little at the ends. And the ones who didn't want double-enders simply squared off one end with what boatbuilders call a transom, which you can see on any rowboat.

Our Southern friend allowed that what we had in mind might take a little longer because it was bigger, but then we'd save time anyway by caulking the seams with stuff that came in cans instead of messing around with tar. Or we could even fasten wooden battens inside seams like some of the real fussy boys on the river. And for sailing, we could just fasten a good-sized fin on the bottom with its middle a little ahead of the middle of the sail and everything would be fine. Anytime we ran into a construction problem, he said, a little bourbon would make everything go together. Bourbon for the boatbuilder, not the boat. Which seemed both pleasant and logical.

So we followed our friend's method and decided *Flying Smelt* should be an 18-footer because that was as long as we could get the wood we could afford. And the width (called the beam) was seven feet because that was as wide as any 18-footer we had seen, and we wanted plenty of comfort room.

As we had been moving like nomads because landlords persisted in selling the houses we rented, we arranged to rent an eighteen-foot piece of real estate for $1 a foot in a boatyard, to build our boat on weekends during the winter when it wasn't snowing. (This is a good arrangement, too, if you live in an apartment, but figure on something like $6 a foot today.)

Although we put in almost four thousand brass screws with a couple of 24-cent screwdrivers from the dime store, we didn't have any problems until the launching, which took place ahead of schedule on a windy Sunday morning, without us. And somebody goofed. When we arrived late in the afternoon, ready to install the cabin's home-built double bunk which was tied on top of the car, the *Flying Smelt,* with our bag of sails in the cabin, was a hundred yards out in the harbor, stuck on a sand bar with the tide rising in a wind that blew my hat off and provided our first opportunity to gather sailing experience. (We reached the boat in our $5 rowing scow, which had not yet been painted.)

In case you plan to become a self-taught sailor, our procedure at that time may be of interest, though some of the steps should be omitted. First, my wife brought the mainsail out of the cabin and began putting it on the mast and boom. (Women are good at this, and less likely than many men to hoist it upside down.) I removed the rudder from the cabin to hang it on the transom pivots, but slipped on the wet deck and fell overboard with it, which rocked the boat considerably. So that when I climbed back aboard with the rudder, we were clear of the sand bar and blowing along freely toward the rocks across the harbor. But we had learned that you can sometimes get a boat off a sand bar by rocking it. You learn by doing.

As soon as we had the rudder in place and the sails up, the mainsail swung all the way out with a bang and we took off at a foaming gallop toward the rocks, which were now much closer. And my wife, who was clinging to the mast, said, "I never thought these things could go so fast, but you'd better steer it."

Our Southern friend had said that sailing was very easy. All you do is aim the boat the way you want to go, and if the wind is behind you let the sail swing all the way out, which it had already done. And if the wind is blowing from the side, just pull the sail in until it stops fluttering. Which I did, and we turned away from the rocks with almost a yard to spare, then picked up speed until we actually began to bounce. My wife came back from the little deck we called the front porch and got into the cockpit before we reached the outer harbor, where the real wham bang began.

When we went past some shore club at the end of the point the *Flying Smelt* was tilted at a very jaunty angle and traveling so fast that the little rowing scow we were towing behind us was standing on its tail like a penguin. There were beautiful little pointed red flags standing straight out from a flagpole on the shore, and all the people on the dock seemed as thrilled as we were as they all waved and yelled, including the man in the club launch.

After we circled around a few times just for the fun of it, we decided to tie the boat to the mooring which the yard man had put out there for us for $5 a few days before.

When we got everything back in the cabin, we waved
back at the man in the launch, who was some distance
away and waving to us with both hands. Then we sat in
our rowing scow and blew into some rushy weeds at the
end of the point, without even having to row.

After we got the car and picked up the scow, we stopped at the bar where we often warmed up after our boat-building sessions, and just missed meeting the man from the launch. The bartender said Tony, who ran the launch, would be a good man for us to know. But he had left after only one drink because he was worn out. He had been chasing around with the launch for hours picking up the club's deck chairs that had blown into Long Island Sound and getting people in from yachts after the gale warnings went up.

We asked what gale warnings were, and he said two pointed red flags, one above the other on the flagpole. But he said the worst part of the whole thing was that when Tony was just about to knock off for the day a couple of lunatics came barreling out of the harbor in the damndest sailboat he had ever seen, with all the sails up in the gale, and not even sense enough to pay attention when everybody in the place was waving and hollering at them to turn back. So Tony had to go out after them, but never caught up. And the rest, he said, we wouldn't believe anyway. But we had learned about gale warnings. (We have since concluded that *Flying Smelt*'s gale performance then and on other occasions was due to her broad beam in proportion to the size of our secondhand sail.)

Once you build a boat the cheap and easy way, you can't help thinking about other kinds of boats you'd like to make the same way. Like the canoe we wanted for our private lake. (Chapter 4.) So we built the canoe one sunny

Saturday, and since then, from time to time, forty other nice little boats, many for magazines. All a little odd, no two alike, most of them sailboats, and some so fast they won races, after we learned about racing. Most of the boats are still sailing.

(One of the things that makes it so simple is stuff called resorcinol resin glue, which was invented years ago for torpedo boats and has been in hardware stores ever since, although lots of people still haven't heard of it. Until it's hard it washes off with water. Next morning it's so tough you can boil your boat to mush, if you're so inclined, without hurting the glue. And if you use it in all joints and seams, you never need to caulk again. But since it's fairly high priced you won't want to waste it. So as soon as you finish the boat, dribble the leftovers into the loose joints of your wobbly furniture.)

Naturally, when you make boat building a habit you often have more boats than you need. We have had them under the porch, on the garage wall, on the ceiling, and finally all over the floor, so the car stayed outside. When you reach this situation you find that, although oddball boats are not always easy to sell, they make nice gifts. But you have to be careful how you present them to people you don't know very well. Like the young couple over at the lake who expressed interest in one of our excess canoes that had a big snarling dragon's head on it. When I said we'd be delighted to give it to them because our garage was so full of boats we even had one in the living room and were building another on the dining-room table, the young woman was delighted and all ready to put the canoe on their car. But her husband gave her a withering look and said, "Can't you see the guy's some kind of nut?"

And that ended it.

If anybody who might later buy your boat watches you building it, don't brag about how easy it is. Lots of people think anything that's easy can't be much good. Always keep a rolled-up blueprint stuck in your belt. Any blueprint. We have one that came with an electric water heater. Pull the blueprint out periodically and take a quick look at it. Then stick it back in your belt, measure some part of the boat, and grunt. This makes you appear very knowledgeable. If you're a real showman, get a dime-store slide rule. These things aren't for measuring, but engineers use them for rough calculations. Just pull the slide partway out, look at it, and say, "Perfect. Absolutely perfect!"

If your audience doesn't know any more about a slide rule than you do, they'll rate you as a whiz kid and speak highly of your boat. So if you can't sell it when you build the next one, you may at least be able to swap it for something. We swapped one with a mechanic for a transmission reseal job, and everybody got a bargain.

The more boats you build, the more boats people think you want. So they tell you about bargain boats they've heard about, which can be intriguing. One of these was a big uninsured yacht that eventually sold for $1 because

Sometimes you find bargain boats like this after a storm. The price on the FOR SALE sign was reduced after it sank, but it's still going strong for its new owner after a little repair work.

it had been stripped by thieves when its owner couldn't afford to have it hauled off the rocks and patched up after a storm. And neither could we. (Today, we could do the job ourselves.) But the lucky buyer was still using it the last time we checked, ten years later. Things like this don't happen often, but they happen. Another involved a cruiser that a storm landed upside down in the driveway of a shorefront home. The homeowner and the boat owner alike were ready to pay to get rid of that one, but we had no place to put it. A new owner with fix-it and bargain-hunting talents had it back on the Sound the following season. If you'd like to find this kind of bargain, let everybody know it. In case you bungle the repair job, an old yacht on your lawn makes a conversation piece and a playhouse for the kids.

If You Want to Try It

While it's not absolutely necessary to pick a simple flat-bottom design like a rowboat for your first boat-building job, it's easier on your nerves. And you'll always have use for the rowboat. You can use it for a tender if you build a schooner later on.

To simplify construction, favor plywood. It's split-resistant, tougher than ordinary wood of the same thickness (about twice as tough), and it minimizes the number of seams. Quarter-inch thickness is adequate for a rowboat.

If you don't like working from plans, simply copy a boat that you have access to when you want to measure something. If you reinforce all joints and seams with resorcinol resin glue, you're likely to turn out a better boat than the one you copy. At least it'll be stronger than an unglued boat, and you won't have to caulk it.

Of course, you can also build a boat from a kit, according to the directions that come with it, and you'll still save plenty. (Look for ads for boat kits in boating magazines.)

These days, however, before you decide what kind of boat you want to build, you'd better get in touch with the Coast Guard and get a copy of all the regulations that now apply to people who want to build their own boats. And all the regulations that apply to the boats. All this deals mainly with how many people the boat can carry and how powerful a motor it can have. And things like identification numbers and life preservers.

Also find out how much you have to pay in your particular state to register your boat if it has to be registered. (State regulations vary.) And if you plan to leave it at a mooring, find out if any mooring space is available, and whether it is likely to cost more than the boat. It's a good idea, too, to find out how many boats have been stolen from wherever you plan to keep your boat. Or maybe plan on a boat you can take to and from the water on top of your car. (In the days of the *Flying Smelt*, boats like that didn't have to be registered, mooring space in our area was free, and in fifteen seasons at the mooring nobody stole the boat.)

If today's boat-building regulations get you down (they really shouldn't), you might be better off buying a boat very cheap, like the sunken one in the photograph. Often you can fix up such a specimen without too much work, the way that one was fixed up by the man who bought it. And if you don't make it look too pretty, nobody's likely to steal it. But, of course, if you build a seventeen-foot three-masted trimaran schooner that you can paddle like a canoe and roll to the water on its nosewheel, like one of ours, nobody's likely to steal that either. Unless you build one of them yourself, it might be hard to explain where you got it.

Wood, Whiskey, and Nails

If you'd like to save something like $50,000 on a $25,000 house that you get for around $3,000, you simply build it yourself. And avoid a quarter century of mortgage payments. But you don't do it the ordinary way. And you should begin with two essentials: a lawyer and liquor. Later you need materials. More about that shortly.

The first step, of course, is acquiring the land on which to build your house. This is where the lawyer comes in, as real estate transactions may vary in the way they're handled, depending on a lot of things, including who does what and where. For example, one big genial man who only wanted a moderate deposit to hold some beautiful land while the paper work was completed told us later that the paper work might take years and that if we wanted the deposit back we could sue. So we hired a fiery lawyer and sat in his office while he called the big genial man, who told him to go to hell. That was where the liquor came in. Our big custom car with the bar in it (Chapter 6) was parked outside the lawyer's office, so we invited him into its rear lobby for a few drinks, as he was in a fury and it was cocktail time anyway. We never did sue the big genial man because it would have cost more than the moderate deposit he said was all he wanted.

After that we undoubtedly looked very grim when we talked to people who wanted to sell land we wanted to buy. For one thing, the two-hundred-acre estate we were renting (Chapter 4) had been sold, which, after the big genial man got through with us, left us only six weeks until moving day. So we developed a land-locating method that worked very well, and could be applied to land hunting in general, which should be kept in mind. We simply drove along small side roads in the country until we got lost, and then asked questions. So, if you want to find land without an agent, get lost. And if you find land you'd like that isn't for sale, take what you can get, so long as you can walk on it without sinking. (There are also many sound and widely published land-judging rules you can follow if you prefer to avoid buying land entirely and still have no regrets.)

The way things worked out, it was a white-haired man talking to a pair of goats in a beautiful meadow who finally solved our problem. The meadow and the goats were his, he said, and would not be sold to anyone, ever, under any circumstances. But the land over on the crossroad was for sale, and the owner lived just up around the bend.

It might be a bargain, the man thought, since nobody had tried hacking a passage into it for years, through the briers and the poison ivy. But he remembered way back when it was a beautiful meadow just like the one he was standing in. Then there was that fourteen head of cattle that went in there to graze, years back, and never came out. Just plumb disappeared. Some folks said there was a fierce underground river back in there, and maybe the cattle somehow dropped into it. And there were others who said the cattle just sank into quicksand. But then, nobody really knew that the underground river was actually there, or the quicksand either. "Only thing that showed was a little stream with a lot of snakes in it. If you could get there to see it."

Later the owner of the land, over a highball in the car, more or less confirmed what the white-haired man had told us, but thought it was a team of horses rather than cattle that had disappeared. And, of course, there were all kinds of things living in there, like raccoons and skunks. And at night if you heard a noise that sounded like a mass murder in progress, it was just the love call of some kind of fox. Best bet, we were told, was to try to cut our way in and see what we thought of it. There was an ax and a scythe at our disposal for the purpose. Just come back up around the bend and pick them up.

As we were still on solid ground after we tunneled our way through the briers for about twenty feet, we decided to end our exploration and return to the car to lift our spirits and weigh the merits of the property. We had already been assured by our lawyer that this particular landowner had a long-established reputation for honesty, and had proved it again by telling him what a terrible time we would probably have getting the land in shape to build on, which coincided exactly with our findings in the brier tunnel. So we bought the property.

The way we looked at it, all we needed was somebody with some kind of a machine to cut a driveway into the place and clear away the brush and the briers. And it didn't take long to find what we needed. One of the men who was surveying the land for us, who had taken a little time out to pick the thorns out of his face, said there was a local farmer about a mile away who could do it. The farmer had a big tractor with a scoop on it that could push its way into the place through the stone wall and then scrape off all the brush.

As it turned out, the man was a sort of combination farmer and contractor, and he did a nice job of pushing a big opening through the wall before he got bogged down in the briers. In fact, he got tangled up so thoroughly that he only accepted half of what we had agreed to pay him. He'd had enough of the whole mess, he said, and just wanted to get away from it, which took about an hour of rocking his tractor back and forth.

Our only problem at that point was that all the lumber for our house was due to arrive from a sawmill at any minute, because it was the cheapest lumber we could get, and we had no place to put it. So we started hacking with our ax and scythe as we had never hacked before. And we were still hacking and becoming limp when the truck arrived. A truck like a fair-sized freight train, and piloted by what appeared to be a giant. He seemed unimpressed by our explanation. All he said was that the lumber was mostly green oak and we'd better cut it and use it while it was still green or we might as well try driving nails into cast iron. As to the briers, he said it shouldn't take more than a couple of minutes to clear them. If we had a Sherman tank. Then he turned his truck, with all its rows of wheels, into the field across the road, yelled to us to get out of the way, and backed into the little notch the tractor had made. In fact, he backed in so mightily that the entire truck disappeared into the briers without a trace except for a terrible roaring and crashing somewhere back in the brush. My wife said we should have told him about the fourteen head of cattle or horses, or whatever they were, but he didn't give us time.

We could see the briers waving and fragments sailing into the air along with chunks of mud and clouds of dust from one end of the place to the other. And suddenly it was all over. The truck lumbered back onto the road empty about fifty yards away and stopped so the giant could step down and pull a small tree from his front bumper. "Next best thing to a Sherman tank," he said. Then he climbed back and drove away.

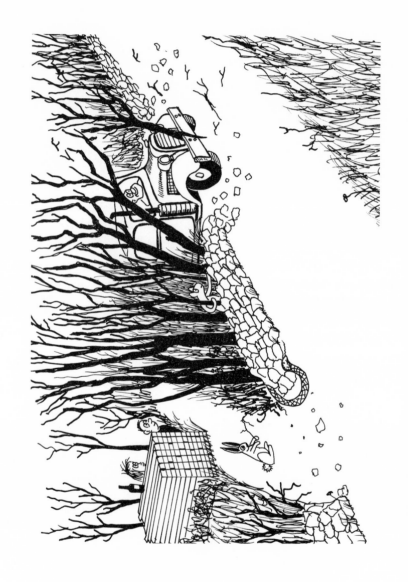

After the dust cleared, we saw our lumber in a neat stack on the flattened tangle that had been briers. And farther back, a little waterfall in the stream where the snakes lived. We learned later that sawmill trucks backed up fast and stopped short to shoot the load of lumber off the back on locust poles that served as rollers. Our mailbox is still mounted on one of the locust poles (which are rot-resistant) twenty years later.

As sawmills can cut your lumber to any thickness you want, you can build your house the way the old-timers did. And it should last just as long, like two hundred years. So look over old barns as well as new houses that are going up. And ask questions.

The sawmill, logically, was built from sawmill lumber in board-and-batten style. If you build that way from green lumber, the sawmill operator told us, you nail the battens to only one side of the seams at first, and nail the other side about six months later, so the wood can shrink without splitting the battens. And it works. But don't forget what the mill's driver said about green oak turning into something like cast iron. The installer who put in our phone broke two screwdrivers mounting the box on the outside wall. And the hunter who fell over our wall with a loaded shotgun that went off as he landed on his face left a part of our garage so full of shot it looked like raisin bread. But without holes.

We also learned that much of the drama and suspense in building a country house comes from the man who

The house we built with the sawmill lumber is 85 feet long, with seven rooms, two baths, air conditioning, patios, waterfalls, and a 1,700-square-foot deck on top—so people are usually surprised to find that it cost less than our car would have cost if we hadn't gotten the car at such a bargain price.

drills your well. He can't tell you in advance whether or not you'll get any water at all. And he can't tell you how far down the water is if it's there. But he can tell you about people who have drilled down hundreds of feet again and again without getting a drop. And as the drilling machine bangs away, you know each foot costs you about the price of a shirt. (Our well hit water at a depth of 125 shirts.)

When we selected our well pump from a mail-order farm catalog, we learned several other important things you should know if you ever do the same thing. First, we found out that the rate of flow from our well was enough to support seven hundred hogs, which, of course, is important if you're a hog farmer. And second, we found that we should not have passed this fact along to anybody, because people out in the country sometimes jump to conclusions.

The man with the white hair and the goats just happened to be talking to us when the well driller told us how many gallons per minute the well could supply. And the first thing we saw in the pump section of the catalog was the chart that matched gallons to hogs, which we thought was amusing enough to mention.

The white-haired man always walked on the other side of the road after that. And we didn't know why until one of our friends from down in Greenwich, who was coming up to have dinner with us, asked somebody along the way if he knew where we lived. And the answer he got was, "If you mean that damned hog breeder, he's at the other end of the road."

The dining room in which we had dinner that night is a monument to the fact that when you're building your own house you can't turn down free materials. We built our dining room around some beautiful interior paneling a friend gave us because it was easier to give it away than install it. In order to provide a room in which to put it,

Hornblower, one of the goats in the group whose owner steered us to our building site, became our daily companion during the building job, even when the goat owner shied away from us because he thought we were hog breeders.

we bought the knocked-down remains of a century-old blacksmith shop for $45 from a local building wrecker and reassembled it to make both a dining room and a studio. Since this formed the most recent part of the house, the newest end is the oldest end—and the end on which we added our garage for $27 because the same wrecker was moving his headquarters. Otherwise the garage might have cost us almost as much as the $45 dining room and studio.

The nice part, architecturally, about building a house this way is that it rambles. Sometimes to a length of eighty-five feet or more, like ours. And it tends to look as if it had always been there. In fact, an old-timer from upstate told us he hadn't seen the place since he was a kid, when his grandfather drove him past it in a 1922 Essex. "It hasn't changed a bit," he said. "Except that you keep your car in the cow shed."

If You Want to Try It

If you want to have a fling at building your own house with your own hands, your best bet is to pick land well out in the country. For one thing, it's likely to be cheaper, if you find the right area, and it's less likely to be bogged down in a maze of regulations made by other people to tell you you're not allowed to build the kind of house you want. We even saw one set of regulations that said you couldn't have a cabinet under your kitchen sink. In any event, get yourself a copy of the local building code if there is one—before you buy. Some of them are based on common sense and some are not.

Naturally, you don't have to build from sawmill lumber. But if there happens to be a sawmill nearby (there are fewer of them than there used to be) and the idea of building with native lumber appeals to you, find out about the prices. Some mills sell lumber only in rough-surfaced form, as it comes from the saw, and others also sell it smoothed, at a higher price. For old-fashioned board-and-batten construction, the rough stuff is fine. Wavy-edged boards just as they come from the log are also used in clapboard fashion.

If you want a more conventional-style house, you'd better use more conventional lumber. And if you really want to do the job in Getting Game style, you'll buy it from a house wrecker, directly at a wrecking site, if possible. When you buy all the lumber from a wrecked house directly at the wrecking site you usually get it cheaper than ever, because the wrecker only has to load it once and unload it once. (If he has to load it at the wrecking job, and unload it at his storage yard, and then reload it to truck it to your site, the extra labor adds to the cost.) If he can't deliver it to your building site because it's too far away, maybe your best bet is a rented truck.

Old barn timbers and barn siding boards at a Connecticut building wrecker's yard. The buildings in the background contain oil burners, furniture, sewing machines, recordplayers, and several laboratory skeletons. All this at the time the picture was taken.

Of course, you can combine new, used, and sawmill lumber. If you use secondhand lumber for the framework of your house, it will be thoroughly seasoned and cut to the sizes used in the house from which it came. Owner-builders often plan their new home accordingly, so it goes together something like an Erector set. Then you can use plywood to save time and work enclosing the framework, and sawmill lumber for siding. Scout all the possibilities before you begin. And add up your costs in advance so that you stay in the Getting Game. The ideal goal: build as much as possible on a pay-as-you-go basis. If you don't have to pay interest, the money you save is your own.

If you decide to build from sawmill lumber, ask lots of questions around the mill and explain what you want to do. Chances are the mill is built the way you want to build, so you can copy the general construction.

If you want to build a conventional house, take a ride to some area where they're being built, look at everything, and ask questions, if you have any. (This beats reading about it, but you can do that too, if your library has an uncomplicated book on the subject.) To keep from being a pest at building sites, you should know the names of the important parts of the house frame, all of which are easy to remember. The upright posts inside the walls are called studs and are usually made of two-by-four lumber. At the bottom, they rest on a horizontal two-by-four called a sole, and at the top they support doubled horizontal two-by-four's called a plate. The big beams that support the floor are the joists, and the ones that support the roof are the rafters, whether the roof slants in two directions, or just one (shed roof) like ours. (The studs, joists, and rafters are spaced evenly in the framework—usually 16 inches apart.) If the walls have two layers of outer covering, the inner one is sheathing (usually plywood or panel-type sheathing board) and the outer one is the siding, like shingle or clapboard.

If you build by old-time barn methods, you use just one good thick layer of vertical siding (typically with battens), which helps support everything, including the roof. Since there are plenty of two-hundred-year-old barns around, some converted to houses, they obviously have what it takes.

After you've spent an hour or so watching the pros put houses together, you'll realize it's not much more involved than building a big doghouse. When you're convinced you can do it, go ahead. If you're timid, start with the

We had to start building in midwinter. So we built the foundation under the house after it was built. (You sometimes have to do this if you buy a house and have it moved to where you want it.) We put the foundation under the house in the spring.

garage. Beginners often do that to get some building experience. If you don't like heavy masonry work, you can hire somebody to build the foundation. (You can also hire a pro to help with anything else.) And, unless you have to have space for a poolroom or a moonshine still, you don't really need a cellar. But decide for yourself. Within a mile of our house there are at least a dozen others with and without cellars built by their original owners, some of whom never built anything before. One liked home building so much he went into the business, made the grade in grand style, and retired while he could still enjoy it.

However and whatever you build in the way of a house, if you've never bought lumber before you're likely to question the sanity of the people who devised the system of lumber sizes. A two-by-four, for example, is really $1\frac{1}{2}$ inches by $3\frac{1}{2}$ inches. The term "two-by-four" is simply a "nominal size." It was 2 inches by 4 inches when it came from the saw. But then it was planed smooth, which made it smaller. And when it was dried it shrank. So nominal 2-inch lumber is always $1\frac{1}{2}$ inches thick. And the width is $\frac{1}{2}$ inch narrower than what it's called—until you get to widths of 8 inches or more, which are $\frac{3}{4}$ inch narrower. And as to nominal 1-inch lumber, it's $\frac{3}{4}$ inch thick.

If you buy lumber from a house wrecker, however, it's likely to be bigger because nominal sizes have been reduced in the past few years. Two inches used to be $1\frac{5}{8}$ inches, and 4 inches used to be $3\frac{3}{8}$. And one inch used to be $\frac{25}{32}$ inch.

But at the country sawmill you have to be

We bought windows for our house from this wrecker's assortment for $7 a dozen, but prices vary.

specific when you ask for something. If you say you want your lumber cut one inch thick and eight inches wide, they may think you really mean it, and you'll get the actual size you ask for. And if you build in barn fashion, that's a good idea.

If there's a local building code where you build, it will usually tell you what size lumber you have to use for the important parts of your house, which is better than guessing. The size of joists and rafters are usually listed according to the span between supports. So you need bigger joists for a wide room. (If there's no code where you build, look for a commonsense code, not one of the silly ones, from somewhere else to serve as a guide. You can usually buy a copy from the building inspector's office or some similar town office.)

The nails you put your house together with come in lengths from one inch to six, though you'll seldom need any longer than four inches. If you're new to nailing, buy your nails according to their length in inches. not by the old traditional "penny sizes," which serve no real purpose and can get you in a state of utter confusion. Under this system a 1-inch nail is a 2-penny nail, a 6-inch nail is a 60-penny nail, and intermediate sizes rate accordingly, such as 8-penny, 10-penny, and so on. The explanation of how all this got started depends on who tells the story. According to one of the logical tales, it generally referred to the price of 100 nails. So you paid only 2 cents for 100 inch-long ones, but you paid 60 cents for 100 six-inchers, which made some sense, but not anymore, since you buy nails by the pound anyway. To avoid headaches, buy your nails

The barn siding for our garage came from this
batch, selected board by board, at the wrecking yard
—after the sawmill burned down.

from a lumberyard or a hardware dealer who
knows something about building. Then you
can explain what you want them for, and
somebody should be able to tell you the size
you need. (Rule of thumb: if you drive a nail
through one piece into another, two-thirds of
the nail should end up in the second place.)

Things like windows and doors come

ready-made in assorted sizes. Just pick what you want at the lumberyard or the house wrecker's. If you mention that you're building your own house, you'll probably be swamped on the spot with information on practically everything in the place.

If you want to do your plumbing and wiring, as many owner-builders do, spend an afternoon in the library with the simplest books you can find on these subjects, and another afternoon looking at the plumbing and wiring in new houses before the interior walls are covered. You'll be happy to learn that house wiring is color-coded to keep you from making mistakes. In most of it you simply connect black wires to brass terminals, white wires to chrome. Or white wires to white wires, black to black. You can see the details in houses being wired. Just be sure you know what to do before you do it.

As to plumbing, you can carry all the plastic pipe for an entire household waste system under one arm, cut it to length with almost any kind of saw, and actually make connections in less than a minute apiece. (If you don't believe it, ask the supplier who sells you the pipe and the fast-setting cement that seals the connections.) Copper water-supply plumbing is almost as easy, as is the cast-iron waste pipe (usually used through the base-

Plumbing fixtures stored behind wrecker's head-quarters. Inside, we found a two-headed calf (stuffed) for $3.50. This is also where our bride friend got her pipe organ, and our neighbor was too squeamish to buy a beautiful automatic range because she was frightened by skulls and a man crawling on the floor with a cannonball.

ment wall and beyond), which once meant heavy work. All of which explains why office workers and concert musicians we know now do their own plumbing and wiring. (It wasn't so easy when we did it.)

If you can remember what you have read

The well driller hit an ample supply of water at a depth of 125 shirts.

in the preceding few pages, you have enough to sound very knowledgeable at cocktail parties when somebody says you're a nut if you think you can build your own house. (The plain fact is that you can, and people should not take pot shots at your self-confidence.) As in boat building (if it happens to be your own cocktail party), keep a blueprint handy, preferably one of some part of a house, with illegible notes scribbled all over it in red pencil. Show it very briefly to skeptics, and with a triumphant look on your face announce that every detail of the job was fully approved by the chief inspector at half past two yesterday afternoon. And, of course, you knew it would be, since the architect who designed it won the Busserman Foundation Trophy three times in the past five years. Then hustle up another round of drinks before somebody asks you what the hell the Busserman Trophy is.

The House
That Came to Dinner

Some years ago we stopped for dinner in a restaurant that served whale steaks and other things that made it very popular. So popular, in fact, that the owner told us he'd like to make the place three times as big as it was. And the next day, when we stopped there for lunch, the place was three times as big. The restaurateur had simply bought a vacant country store about a mile away and had it moved up against his restaurant, after which a carpenter nailed the two together and connected them with a doorway. As simple as that.

If you're house hunting, think about this sort of thing. About five miles from that restaurant a dozen $20,000 houses that had to be cleared out of the path of a new highway were sold for $900 apiece and moved. Once moved, the houses were the same. Only the addresses were changed.

If you already have a house that's not quite big enough, maybe you can do what the restaurateur did. We bought a little old blacksmith shop and added it to our house to make a studio for less than $100. (Details in Chapter 8. It might cost around $500 now.)

Naturally, you don't find unwanted vacant houses just everywhere. But it pays to look. Sometimes a fine old home happens to be on a large tract of land where some developer wants to build rows of modern houses, all alike. So the old one has to go. At other times, old houses must go to reduce somebody's taxes. So when you see a place that looks deserted or haunted in an area where you'd like to live, ask questions. Maybe you can match up a piece of land you can afford with a house that's free, or almost free, and save yourself a quarter century of mortgage payments. We just missed getting a free barn simply because we didn't ask about it. So the bulldozer got it.

At times, you can find unwanted houses in the local newspaper. It's news, for example, if a large number of houses have to be cleared for some state or federal brainstorm. And the classified ads sometimes offer small cottages or sheds free to save the owner the cost of hiring somebody to take them away. (You're not likely to find free barns today because of the demand for barn siding and timbers.)

However you locate your take-away building, you'll have some checking to do before you buy, or even close a deal to accept it for nothing. There are situations where even

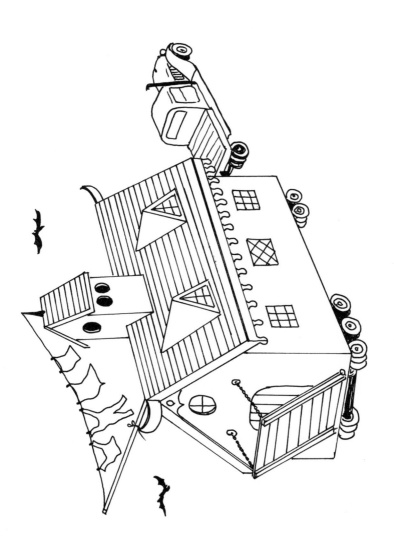

a free house isn't a bargain, as when you can't move the house because it's thirty feet high and has to go under a railroad bridge that's only fifteen feet high.

A more common problem than bridges is utility wires. If they have to be taken down and put up again in order to let your haunted house pass by, you get the bill. So drive along all roads that lead from the house you plan to move to the place where you want to put it, and look for utility wires that cross the road. And look to see if your house has to go under the wires to get onto your property. Before you give up, no matter what you find, get an estimate from a building mover. (The nearest one listed in the yellow pages makes a good beginning.) He knows things about the game you don't know, some of which may be pleasant. And he knows about things like permits, which vary in nature and price, but usually are within reason. And, of course, he can give you some kind of estimate on the job.

But before you do all this, walk through the house to make sure you'd like it if you had it. Never mind the lawn and the water supply and the septic tank. You can't take them with you. But check with the local building inspector on what's needed where you intend to plant the house. Also tell him what you plan to do, and ask if there's some horrible reason why you shouldn't. The people who will be your new neighbors can tell you about other things like taxes in the area, and the politics. If you approach them genially. In case your children are frightful, ill-mannered, brutal shin-kickers, leave them home. And if the mere mention of taxes and the local political structure sends your prospective neighbors into a cursing, screaming fury, maybe things will be better five or ten miles away, which is in easy house-moving distance. A few extra miles doesn't usually affect the moving cost too much. The big part of the job is getting the house on and off the wheels.

The house mover can also do something for you that developers don't do: he can set your house to face in any direction you want it to face. Look down almost any development street and you'll see that all the houses face the street and all are the same distance from the street. Because it's customary. So if the street runs east and west, all the houses on one side have sunny front rooms and all the ones on the other side have sunless front rooms. If you have your house moved to your property and you have a determined and courageous point of view, you can have the only house on the road with the back facing front. If you happen to like that particular exposure. (Older-style homes in open country often face the driveway instead of the road to take advantage of sunlight at different times of the day.) Many home owners have hired a house mover to simply lift their house up, turn it around to a better position, and put it down again on a suitably altered foundation. Others have had houses moved from one part of the property to higher ground on another part so as to have a better view.

And there are those who have had their houses moved

out of congested areas into the surrounding country for assorted reasons. If, for example, the town fathers' revised zoning code results in a slaughterhouse and a glue factory rising across the street from you where the tree-lined park used to be, you may prefer a new location. Even a recreation center with a driving range on the street behind you can be a problem if you occasionally get hit in the mouth with a golf ball. (It has happened.)

Ordinarily, if your house isn't taking a really long trip, you don't have to worry too much about disturbing your daily routine. You leave for work in the morning from Slaughter Street and come home to your new address on Outer Gooseberry Road. In one instance, a homeowner bedded down with flu simply stayed in bed while his house moved across town. In a mere matter of hours you can leave behind the clatter of the city with its staggering taxes for the country sounds of roaring power mowers and minibikes and screaming children. So it's not surprising that some houses are moved more than once. One city museum was moved three times, twice by the same building mover. Which shows that it pays to choose your destination with care. In case you stay.

In the summer you can have a waiting foundation built by a contractor who tailors it to your migrant house. So you land like a yacht docking at a marina, and connect to the plumbing and wiring. In winter, you may have to spend your time at a motel while your house waits on timber piers for the spring thaw. But you don't have to

This house was a real bargain, though at first glance it might not look it. It didn't have to travel far—up the same road to a new site.

pay for furniture storage. It's usually less bother to move your house with the furniture in it than to move the furniture without the house. You don't have to pack anything in cartons or worry about somebody scratching your Duncan Phyfe, or even spilling the martini you left on the bar.

Of course, there may be work to be done on the house after it arrives, as in the case of a commercial henhouse that friends of ours converted to a cozy Cape Cod of showplace quality at a new location. And it was ready to occupy before the month was over, as moved buildings often are. In fact, a house moved years ago in upper New York farm country carried a sizable pot of pigs' knuckles and sauerkraut simmering on an oil stove, which timed out ready and tender when the house settled on its new foundation and we joined the owners for dinner. Which shows that it can be done. If you like pigs' knuckles.

If You Want to Try It

If you own property and plan to build, ask questions and take a good look around the surrounding area to check the possibility of finding a bargain house that could be moved to your land. It might cost you a lot less than building a new house, if there are no complications involved in the moving job. Needless to say, you may not find such a house. But if there is one, it's much better to find it before you build than after.

If the house you plan to move is in good shape when you find it, the chances are it'll be in good shape after it's moved. On most moving jobs, even the goldfish aren't disturbed.

Some of the best bargains, however, are

old houses in obviously neglected shape. If you're tool-handy, you can probably do all or a major part of the restoration work yourself. The house with the shed roof over the front door is a good example of one of these neglected bargains. It was moved to a new site along the same road, and is now a neighborhood showplace.

If you're worried about things like termites, you can have a specialist look the house over before you buy. (You'll usually find people like this not too far away; check under "Exterminating and Fumigating" in the yellow pages of the local phone book.)

If you're operating on a shoestring and can't afford specialists, look the place over yourself from the bug standpoint. You can tell a termite from an ant by the fact that an ant has a skinny waistline and a termite has a thick one. And there are other things about termites you can learn in the library. If, for example, you find a pile of insect wings without insects somewhere in the house, they may belong to termites—which shed their wings before eating a house at certain times. But the mere presence of termites doesn't mean all is lost, or even that the termites are alive. They may not have done any serious damage yet. But if you borrow a library book to learn how to get rid of them, don't keep it it in the house. Termites also occasionally eat books. Since the building mover will have to look the house over (along with the route it must travel) before you buy, ask him to check the termite possibilities too. He's likely to have a keen eye in that field.

One of the things you can check yourself is the foundation of the house. If it's a good solid cemented stone job, it may make the moving job cost a little more because the building mover has to work harder to break out sections of it in order to get his timbers under the house so he can move it. But don't worry about it. Crumbly stone foundations with loose mortar and masonry-block foundations (which can be broken with a sledge) are quicker and easier.

At the destination of the moved house, the best bet is, of course, a waiting foundation built to fit. But if you can't arrange this in time, the building mover can plant your bargain house on temporary piers of timber so you can have a mason build the foundation under it later. If you're in this sort of situation, ask the house mover all about it in advance. In fact, ask him every question that comes to your mind, including the name of a good mason.

As some of the best house bargains are really pretty much of a mess, it's essential to know just how much of a mess is still a bargain. In general, if the wood isn't seriously bug-eaten or rotted, things look hopeful. If the inside plastered walls have had big holes smashed in them (gnat-brained vandals seem to enjoy doing this), don't lose any sleep over it. If it's an old house it probably has no insulation inside the walls, so you'd have to remove the inside walls anyway if you wanted to install in-the-wall insulation. Also, if you have psychological hang-ups and would like to vent your pent-up fury on something, smashing away at the walls can be sheer delight. (If they're plaster, you'll also have to smash away the laths.) In the end, after you've eliminated the inside walls, you buy rolls of fiberglass insulation and staple it in place. (You can usually borrow or rent the stapler where you buy the insulation. This is also a good place to ask questions.)

If your bargain is a real oldie with a leaky roof, ask the house mover about a good roofer. Before the roofer comes (if he's booked up for a long time ahead) you can save the day by covering the roof with stuff called "roll roofing." You nail it on according to the instructions on the wrapper around the roll, and seal the seams with roofing cement, which you buy in the same place. And, of course, you ask questions.

If you do any or all of the roof work yourself, play it safe. Tie a husky safety rope around your middle, and drape it up over the peak and down to a firm knot that holds it to something substantial like a tree. Plan the length of the rope so you can't roll far enough down the roof to fall off the edge. And have a helper to hand you the things you forgot to take up on the roof.

Once your moved house is settled on its foundation, you can get around to the plumbing and wiring. But you should know the regulations in the area before you have your house moved. Since you'll need a lawyer for the legal aspects of the whole affair, let him tell you what you need to know about the regulations. The powers that be may tell you just where you can put such things as septic tanks and wells (if you need a well). If you have a pro build the foundation before the house gets there, be sure he leaves openings (or can arrange to cut them) for all the pipes that have to go through foundation walls.

There's always the chance that somewhere along the line of smashing out the inside walls you'll discover a beautiful cache of fine old table silver. It has happened. Just be glad you didn't find a cache of revolvers. That has happened too.

The City Dump
and Other Treasure-Trove

As you progress as a player of the Getting Game, don't be afraid to try new sources, like the city dump. If you think your social circle might consider this inelegant, just keep quiet about it. And take pride in your work, like a friend of ours who glories in the fact that whenever he buys a new car he goes to his local city dump for a free pair of extra wheels for his snow tires. And the bike that lured him away from jogging came from the same dump. Which gives you some idea of what a good, uninhibited scrounger can expect to find. But, of course, the protocol that must be followed varies from dump to dump, many of which are so exclusive you can't get in unless you are a local resident. Once you are in the dump, however, plan your free shopping so as not to interfere with the

bulldozers. That way the operators will know you really belong. But beware of dumps with NO TRESPASSING or NO PILFERING signs.

If you live in a metropolitan area, scrounging around the dump may be taboo as well as impractical. But there is usually another, more feasible procedure that has been used by many Getting Game players. This consists of keeping a careful watch on things beside trash cans along the street for pickup by refuse trucks. If you find something you like, you can save the trash collector the trouble of loading it on his truck. But before you trot off with your free prize, be sure it's being discarded, not just transferred from one building to another. This precaution is essential to keep you out of the pokey.

Acquiring furniture and other things in this manner eliminates the stigma of having found it in the city dump. You can tell everybody, including yourself, that it was the kind of bargain you don't find in the big stores. The place where you got it was on a side street, and since the price was right, you grabbed it. This much is usually true. If you don't say any more. And if you feel you must say more, pass your hand fondly along the surface of your prize and murmur, "Genuine *robbaccia*." Which sounds imported, adds status, and means trash.

The important point is fortitude. Don't let mere terms like "city dump" steer you away from possible treasures. Discreetly maintain a scavenger outlook wherever you go, and you are likely to discover all sorts of free things

New horizons. The vast wasteland of the city dump is usually departmentalized for your browsing convenience. The label on the old tank tells you that this part is for all garbage. So you pass it up for the more intriguing and useful junk area.

that other people don't even notice, which puts you in a class with some famous industrialists. More than one manufacturing genius has made productive use of the crates in which his suppliers ship things.

Which brings up the matter of where you buy your liquor. If you have never gone to a liquor store for lumber or furniture, you have been missing opportunities. You can often get beautifully grained lumber in sizes lumber-yards don't stock, and, of course, it's free. Or you may prefer to consider it furniture that requires only a small amount of work to give it the luxurious touch. The marble-topped cabinets we have in various parts of our house, for example, were originally wooden liquor cases, which makes perfect sense, as they still contain liquor. But you don't have to buy a case of liquor to get the case. Just let your regular liquor dealer know you want the cases, and let his other customers buy the contents, which may take a little time.

Unfortunately, many distillers now ship their wares in corrugated cardboard cartons, so the liquor-store lumber supply is more limited. But some imported wines and liquors still come in wooden cases. If you happen to locate enough of them, you can do what we did a few years back, when most Scotch whisky was shipped in wooden cases. We simply took several dozen of them apart and used them to cover our otherwise dull studio ceiling with assorted brand names that looked very mellow after a coat of varnish.

From the cases that still had intact lids, we made handsome little marble-topped cabinets. If you look in the yellow pages under "Marble" you can usually find somebody who sells polished marble tiles of the type you see on the walls of office-building lobbies. For your fancy cabinetwork on liquor cases, use tiles that are either eight by twelve inches or a foot square. Just cut a piece of wood the same size and nail it to one end of the liquor case, lay the marble on it, and add a rim of any kind of lumberyard molding around it. If you don't know how to use molding, have a picture framer make you a frame to fit around the marble. This can be even fancier.

Use the liquor cases, stained with a little gravy coloring, or decorated as your artistic talents permit, to make little marble-topped cellarets, and you save enough to buy the liquor. All of which results in more fun than buying finished cellarets.

If you have a rip-roaring nature, leave the liquor case just as it is, with labels exposed. Just varnish it so it won't snag some special guest's nylons. With the box standing on end, the lid can be hinged as a door. (If you can hang a picture, you can do this.) If your rugs are thick and mushy, put molding or casters under the case so the door won't scrape the carpet pile.

For a more conservative effect you can tap the liquor

case apart gently and put it back together inside out, like the ones in the photograph, so the labels don't show. Then anytime you want to brag about how you made the thing, all you need do is open the cabinet door and show people the label. Or you can make up a tale about how the president of the distilling company had the cabinets made up as gifts for his more distinguished customers.

To produce an attractive depth of tone before you varnish the thing you can either brush on some walnut stain or use some of the stuff cooks use to give a deep brown color to pale gravy. If you haven't got some in your kitchen you can get it in any supermarket. Just dilute it to the tone you want or use it straight. What's left you can always use in the gravy.

One warning is essential if you start collecting liquor cases: drive straight home after you put them in your car. If you park somewhere and go shopping there's always a chance that some character who has an urgent need for liquor may think the cases are full. (People like this are not always keen observers.) This happened to us, with the result that we had to replace a window in our Edsel after the break-in.

With all the money you save (and you really can save a lot) by exploring dumps and making rich-looking furniture from liquor cases, you can actually buy some expensive things, if you do it on the same tight-fisted basis. Things like solid gold jewelry with big flawless diamonds. And lavish watches and cameras and other things you won't find at the house wrecker's or the city dump. For things like these, try your nearest pawn shop. The proprietor is likely to be an expert at estimating value because his business depends on it. And, because of the way it works, some of his wares may be new (bought for resale), some secondhand. But, to keep things moving, bargains are the rule. Like the $150 TV we bought for $50 and used without repairs for four years. And the grand old Zeiss lens we bought for $15 and used to make more than seven thousand prints, including the ones in this book. If you don't find what you want in one of these places— maybe a hi-fi or a mink coat—you'll probably find it in another. If you've never bought anything in a pawn shop, try it. You'll like it.

Naturally, in the normal course of events, you'll sometimes have to buy something from a conventional source because your offbeat sources can't supply it. To approach this in Getting Game fashion, begin by checking the yellow pages for suppliers of the thing you want to buy. And to save time, do your initial shopping by phone, which lets you compare prices, and can be very educational too.

Using this method, a friend of ours who wanted a distinctive anniversary present for his wife found (by calling under listings for candy and fur) that for about the same expenditure, he could surprise her with either a mink stole or two thousand pounds of jellybeans, both of which she likes very much. After also checking the leather category

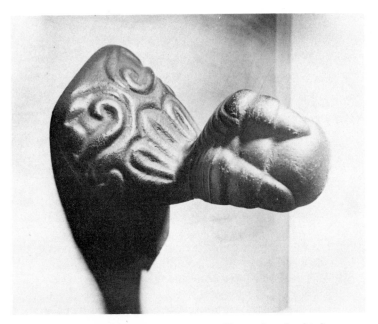

One of our African primitives—old cast-iron bathtub
leg from a house wrecker. This one cost 25 cents.

he decided on the stole plus ten pounds of jellybeans in a
custom-made handbag of the finest slunk, which he had
learned was the costly skin of unborn calf, tanned with
the hair on it. Very silky hair. Understandably, his wife
was impressed.

Our friend followed the basic Getting Game rule of
asking questions, which is how we happened to find out
about slunk and the high esteem in which it is held. And it
was from the leather supplier who happened to have the

A young newlywed homeowner salvaged a set of metal kitchen cabinets from this heap. The mere fact that something lands on the dump doesn't mean it's useless. It merely means that somebody had no use for it, in most cases, and couldn't sell it. If you shop the dump console yourself with the thought that you are a conservationist in your own way.

slunk in stock that he learned where to get the bag custom made. All of which illustrates how you can gather a wide range of information about different aspects of a business from people in almost any part of it. As another instance, if our friend had not asked his jellybean supplier, he would never have known that he didn't have to take his ten pounds in assorted colors, but could have them all black, which his wife preferred, for the same price. (This is now a common practice in the jellybean industry.) In fact, he could have had two thousand pounds of them, all black.

Demonstrating once again why Getting Game players get more satisfaction for each dollar spent.

The same general system also enables you to find things most people never think about. Like the time we wanted some big blocks of neoprene to remount our boat motor so it wouldnt vibrate ripples over the surface of the martinis. (If you ask your friends, you'll usually find that none of them knows where to get big blocks of neoprene.) All we did was look under "Rubber" in the yellow pages of a metropolitan-area phone book, and we found a place that sent us the blocks the next day for much less than we thought things like that would cost. If you can't find what you're looking for in the yellow pages, there are big multi-volume business registers you can buy for about the price of a good tire, which list makers and suppliers of almost everything all over the country. Or you can look at them in your public library. (We once found a supplier of straitjackets in one of these for a friend who was trying to duplicate the escape tricks of Harry Houdini. As with neoprene blocks, you'll find most of your friends don't know where to buy straitjackets.)

To make the most of secondhand shops as a bottom-price source of furniture you can brag about, visit a number of very fancy furniture and antique shops first. And if you find what looks like identical furniture in each one, at prices hundreds of dollars apart and hundreds of dollars beyond your budget, rejoice. Since you're not going to buy it anyway, there's no reason to worry about why some lavish furniture costs more than other lavish furniture. But it happens. What's important is that you have some idea of what to say you paid for the same style of furniture when you buy it later at a secondhand store for pocket money. (Where possible, try sticking to a well-known antique style.) If it looks as if it had seen better days, simply say it's been in the family for years. And underplay it a little. It's not real Duncan Phyfe, of course. Just a reproduction by Ezra Gilhooly, who worked for Phyfe from 1798 to 1811. Your aunt, who bought the stuff, was, of course, a Gilhooly, On her father's side.

At times, too, you may even buy something brand-new without relinquishing your Getting Game concept. Possibly at some giant department store in the midst of the greatest sale in the company's history, since last year. If you have compared prices, you can often win at this sort of thing, although you may face a problem if you try to do what comes naturally, the way you might do it at your favorite house wrecker's. Like the time we found a ladder-back chair at the right price in one of New York's big famous department stores, and handed the salesman the money and said we'd take the thing with us, as we had a car waiting.

We knew immediately from the expression on his face and the way his mouth began to quiver that we had thrown a wild curve. What we wanted to do, he said, just wasn't done. There was no need to do it since the store had three different easy-payment plans plus charge accounts that made cash unnecessary, and also free delivery. And that particular chair wasn't even on sale, and was on display besides. The ones up on the dais were what we should have because they had been drastically reduced for the great sale that was then going on.

We pleaded that we didn't care whether the chair we wanted was on sale or on display or even shopworn because the red seat cushion with the little yellow butterflies and the blue lima beans would go much better with the drapes in our kitchen than would the bile-green cushions with the purple chipmunks up on the dais.

We discovered, however, that this sort of situation often cannot be resolved at the sales level, sometimes because there is no suitable printed form to fill out that would cover it. But it can usually be handled "upstairs" if you happen to be in a store with its top executive offices in the same building. In the end we won, and took the chair with us. Which is worth remembering in case you shop the big department stores.

Things are different now, of course, thanks to modern computerization. When one of our neighbors ordered a nine-by-fifteen blue carpet to be delivered the following Wednesday, every dimension, date, and detail were fed into the store's computer system for delivery and billing. The same store where we bought our chair. But the bill arrived without a carpet.

When our neighbor complained, he was told to return the bill immediately for reprocessing. On the following

Wednesday he received a fifteen-by-twenty beige carpet without a bill. So in the long run, things tend to equalize. More or less. And the way our neighbor looked at it, what's the use of constantly complaining. Even though years have passed and the bill never came.

How to Lie About a Buy

When you have mastered the Getting Game you can, and usually do, have more for less than other people. But don't rub it in. Learn to fib in a kindly way that also accounts for things that might be difficult to explain.

For example, a hardworking citizen who has just had a garage built for $2,000 doesn't want to hear that you got a bigger one for $27. (We have the $27 one.) And people don't enjoy knowing that you furnished your entire living room, complete with newly unholstered period chairs, marble-topped tables, bookcases, cabinets, grand piano, wall-to-wall carpeting, and custom-designed lamps, for less than they paid for a discount sofa. So don't tell them. Also, for many folk, a beautiful thing loses its glamour unless they think it cost a fortune. So don't gloat. Lie modestly.

Imaginary relatives gave you some of your handsome possessions. You have a cousin in the carpet business. You get things through interior decorator friends with foreign names like Enrico Manicotti. You met him at a cocktail party when he came to the States in '65 to redo the Pomeranian Embassy. Great fellow. Beautiful wife. Damn good tennis player—almost wore you out. But he got you some gorgeous stuff. Made you keep quiet about the price. Wonderful.

If it's an individual piece, credit the cabinetmaker and build a positive background. It's a real Schuetz-Maybach. The elder Schuetz, from Friedrichshafen. His son became burgomeister of Iltz. Fellow from the furniture association showed you the Schuetz-Maybach signature on the bottom of the thing. Not many of them around. The Secretary of State has one. Your antique dealer probably never knew what it was. You wouldn't have known either if it hadn't been for the fellow from the furniture association.

If the thing has an Early American look about it, like the hutch in our living room, fashion the background to suit it. Nobody would believe the truth about this one anyway, as it was made from the wood of four Scotch whisky cases, some shelves we took out of a kitchen cabinet, and the end we sawed off the dinner table that was too big for our dining room. But it has an authentic antique appearance because the door pulls came from a seventy-five-year-old sewing machine.

So people sometimes ask about it because it seems a

little odd, and we treat the queries lightly. Just an old Krellwood-Duncan, we tell them, not worth much, but a good, sound example, even though we don't know which one of the brothers designed it. And, of course, we would never pay what they're asking for them now. We simply don't think any hutch that size is worth a thousand dollars.

If it's a house that you've built, and it has a past-era atmosphere about it, like ours, try a historic background. And make it reasonably confusing. The main part of the house was Colonel Crankwell's headquarters during the Fescue uprising. But it was moved from the old Colby farm about eighty years ago, and there were some alterations made. You don't read much about the uprising in the average history book because it lasted only four hours, and the British fled to Secaucus.

If you have a photograph of your great-grandfather, hang it on the wall, framed, and say it's the only genuine picture of Colonel Crankwell you've ever been able to locate. A fine man. You hate to think about his having to eat his own horse during that awful winter. But it actually led to one of the biggest industries in the state. The whole story is covered in Birdly's "Early Americana," Fourth Edition. Beautifully written. But, sorry to say, you've lent your only copy of Birdly's to a neighbor who owns the old Crankwell barn.

In order to avoid any impression that you are a scrounger or a scavenger, never let anyone forget that you are a perfectionist. The knobs that don't match on your double doors were made to order for you at considerable expense, the identical type of mismatched knobs that were on those doors at the time Crankwell's first son was born. The old cast-iron bathtub legs you bought at the scrap-metal yard for 50 cents apiece and painted black to use as doorstops are genuine African primitives. Not many around. Yours are the work of Hakin Abdul Agwab, who was commissioned to create them for an Arabian sheik who had them cast in Pottstown. The foundry foreman made a few bucks on the side turning out extra ones for art collectors, which is how you got them.

Always be ready, too, with distracting remarks in case any part of your house or its Getting Game furnishings has some perceptible flaw that can't be readily explained. If you notice anybody looking intently at a crack in your wall plaster, you announce that he is standing on the same floorboards that Caruso stood on when he sang *Pagliacci* with such volume that his voice broke four windows in the old Metropolitan Opera House. The cracked window in your kitchen is, of course, from the opera house. You bought it along with the boards when the building was torn down. Worth a small fortune now to opera buffs. You even have the actual needle and thread that were used to stitch up the great Tetrazzini's dress when it split right in the middle of the second act.

Naturally, the deep inner charm of the distinctive items

you have collected often lies in the story behind them. Not for all the world would you allow anyone to repolish the dull marble on the quaint table with the cracked legs. It was one of the last to be made at the only factory in Bavaria that turned out that particular style. A family enterprise run by Horst something or other. Poor man ran amuck and blew the place up just as you were driving by in a rented Citroën. The table landed right in front of you and cracked two of the legs, creating a driving hazard which you removed and now have in your living room.

Your nine-year-old power cruiser is one of the famous SQ 500 series, fastest model the company ever built. Seven knots faster than the new line, but then the company has been going downhill ever since they fired old Cliff Toppler, greatest engineer they ever had. This permits an immediate distraction in case some avid boating fan starts pressing you for details on the SQ 500 series. You plunge into dissertation on the outrageous way they treated old Cliff Toppler just because some blonde ad model took all her clothes off, the same way she always did when you knew her back in Cicero. After all, Toppler was supposed to run an engineering department, not a vice squad.

Engraved brass plates like the ones you see under paintings in the art museums are, of course, more convincing than mere spoken words. You order them from jewelers at a few dollars per plate and so many cents per word—like telegrams, but more expensive. A brass plate inscribed with the words "Built for the First Duke of Dellycroft, by Cedric Crackleton" can add greatly to the importance of almost anything wooden that you build from a kit. Just be sure it has a dreary finish and plenty of dents in it. The same kind of brass plate can also credit your antiquated power boat with winning the first race from the Delaware Water Gap to the North Sea at a sustained speed of seventy-one knots. You can always explain that there was some refueling en route, and that the engine has been replaced since. And of course, they don't make them the way they did then.

As you gain experience at lying about your acquisitions, you will tend to believe the things you say, which makes you much more convincing. And you will be able to apply the same methods to other household problems, like the weekender who arrives uninvited with persistent regularity. After he has enjoyed a fruit compote with some luscious kumquats in it, you tell him the kumquats were the greatest bargains you have found in a long time. You picked them up about three weeks ago for only five cents a jar. They were supposed to have been smashed and buried in a six-foot-deep trench and covered with quicklime. Just because they came from the kitchen of the Hospital for Contagious Diseases that was closed after the cholera outbreak. But you made a deal with one of the ditchdiggers. Your cousin, Pete, bought a bunch of them too. Which reminds you that you've been meaning to phone Cousin Pete. Last week when you called he couldn't come to the phone because the doctor was checking him over to try to find out why he was covered all over with purple blotches that seemed to be making his hair fall out.